MW00358366

Harbors of
Cape Cod
& the Islands

Arthur P. Richmond

Schiffer Publishing Ltd®

4880 Lower Valley Road Atglen, Pennsylvania 19310

Acknowledgments

No book of this scope is possible without the assistance of numerous people.

To the nameless, friendly local natives who pointed me in the right direction for the next shot. It's amazing what is around the next corner.

To my editors, Tina Skinner and Doug Congdon-Martin, for their support, motivation, and encouragement in this project.

To Tony Pane, for his apt guidance and knowledge.

To Chuck Edgar, and the fantastic flights over Cape Cod.

To Bob Ziniti, for his computer assistance.

To Randy and Pat Bartlett, for their knowledge of gunk holing on Cape Cod

To Nicole and Brandi, thanks for the support and inspiration.

To Carol, for her endless support and guidance.

To Doug and Jared, thanks.

To Salty, my new best friend.

Copyright © 2008 by Arthur P. Richmond
Library of Congress Control Number: 2008922897

All rights reserved. No part of this work may be reproduced or used in any form or by any means—graphic, electronic, or mechanical, including photocopying or information storage and retrieval systems—without written permission from the publisher.

The scanning, uploading and distribution of this book or any part thereof via the Internet or via any other means without the permission of the publisher is illegal and punishable by law. Please purchase only authorized editions and do not participate in or encourage the electronic piracy of copyrighted materials.

"Schiffer," "Schiffer Publishing Ltd. & Design," and the "Design of pen and ink well" are registered trademarks of Schiffer Publishing Ltd.

Covers and Book Designed by: Bruce Waters
Type set in Souvenir Lt Bt

ISBN: 978-0-7643-3007-0 Printed in China

Schiffer Books are available at special discounts for bulk purchases for sales promotions or premiums. Special editions, including personalized covers, corporate imprints, and excerpts can be created in large quantities for special needs. For more information contact the publisher:

Published by Schiffer Publishing Ltd.
4880 Lower Valley Road
Atglen, PA 19310
Phone: (610) 593-1777; Fax: (610) 593-2002
E-mail: Info@schifferbooks.com

For the largest selection of fine reference books on this and related subjects, please visit our web site at **www.schifferbooks.com**
We are always looking for people to write books on new and related subjects. If you have an idea for a book please contact us at the above address.

This book may be purchased from the publisher.
Include $3.95 for shipping.
Please try your bookstore first.
You may write for a free catalog.

In Europe, Schiffer books are distributed by
Bushwood Books
6 Marksbury Ave.
Kew Gardens
Surrey TW9 4JF England
Phone: 44 (0) 20 8392-8585; Fax: 44 (0) 20 8392-9876
E-mail: info@bushwoodbooks.co.uk
Website: www.bushwoodbooks.co.uk
Free postage in the U.K., Europe; air mail at cost.

Contents

Foreword

When this project of writing a book and taking photographs of the harbors of Cape Cod and the Islands was first presented to me, I thought this should be relatively straightforward and not too difficult. Little did I realize what would be involved in the project.

I don't know if most people read the foreword, but I'm going to explain how I put this book together and what resources I used to produce the final project. Read this and you'll understand the steps involved. First, this book would not have been possible without the endless, nameless people who answered questions, provided directions to out of the way places, and explained the uniqueness of a certain place or harbor. After making a list of the major harbors, I had to decide in what order I should put them. I thought, "why not show them chronologically based on their discoveries?" Gosnold may have visited Provincetown before, but he actually started a settlement on Cuttyhunk in 1602 (albeit for less than a month before returning to England). Therefore, I started with Cuttyhunk, then P'town, and continued west towards the canal.

In the introduction, I have also included a brief discussion of the geology of the Cape and the last ice age, which was responsible for its landforms. Some awareness of this geology is necessary to enable the questioning observer to understand the changes that are constantly occurring. No discussions or photographs are complete without an understanding of these physical alterations. I have also included a brief synopsis of the early human history of the Cape. Neither of these discussions is extensive, but numerous resources are available for those interested in further research on either subject (*see the bibliography*).

Once I had an outline, I had to decide what images to include. Harbor pictures that included some vessels, some characteristic activities of that harbor, and some picturesque or off-season shots were fairly straightforward choices. Having photographed the Cape for over thirty years, I have a large source of images that could be used. All the images in the book are mine. But, what about Prince Cove, or the other harbors that I didn't have an image of? A road trip was necessary to shoot those out of the way places, and for an aerial shot of a harbor, to get a better perspective, I rented a helicopter and flew around the cape. Then, I thought, what did these places look like years ago? So, I collected some old postcards for some of the more popular harbors. After that, I went to NOAA, and perused their archival files for old charts in order to show how harbors change. No harbor is an entity unto itself, so I have included the lighthouses that stand to guide mariners into those respective places. Many people will sit by harbors and watch the goings on, so I have included some of the common birds that the casual onlooker might see and wonder about. All the bird images are mine. All the birds pictured in this book are commonly found on the Cape and can be seen in many of the harbors. I have tried to capture the major harbors and waterways of Cape Cod and any not included are my error of omission.

For each town, I have included the harbor's location, a brief maritime history and any events of significance that I could discover, as well as the present status of the waterways. I hope you enjoy the book as much as I have had in putting it together.

Geological History

Any discussion of Cape Cod's harbors must begin thousands of years ago with the geologic forces that formed this spit of land jutting into the Atlantic. Mainland Massachusetts was formed in excess of 300 million years ago and is known for its rock-strewn fields and gently rolling hills of granite and bedrock. Cape Cod, on the other hand, has no bedrock and is only sand, gravel, clay, and the occasional glacial erratic.

About one million years ago, the earth was becoming cooler, and forces in the great ice sheets were developing that would eventually scrape and scar the New England landscape to form Cape Cod, Martha's Vineyard, Nantucket, the Elizabeth Islands, and even Long Island, New York. In the beginning, more snow fell during the year than melted and glaciers were formed. For hundreds of thousands of years, ice up to two miles thick slowly advanced and receded across the landscape; but it was only in the last fifty to seventy thousand years, during the Pleistocene Epoch, that the topography that we now recognize as the Cape and islands was formed. Slowly oozing forward, this sheet of ice formed several lobes, pushing rocks and soil along the front edge of the glacier and producing the distinctive geography formed by the Buzzards Bay Lobe, which created the Elizabeth Islands and the western coast of Cape Cod, which is significantly rockier than the rest of the peninsula. The Cape Cod Bay Lobe and the South Channel Lobe, pushing south, created and formed the Cape. Each lobe deposited the glacial till it had scraped from the land farther in the north.

Then, about twelve thousand years ago, the climate warmed and the ice sheets started to melt and lose their thickness. As more water was added to the oceans, Martha's Vineyard and Nantucket were surrounded by water and became islands. As the glaciers receded, the ocean tides and waves would determine the shapes these land masses would take. They are still at work today, constantly changing and modifying the shoreline. It is also possible to see the results left by the glacier. The forward edge of the ice sheet, or terminal moraine, is the highest land on the Cape and extends from Cuttyhunk north to Sandwich and east to Orleans where it can be seen in the bluffs behind Nauset Beach. Throughout the region, kettles, or round depressions, were formed where large blocks of ice remained, surrounded by the till deposited by the glacier. When the ice finally melted, ponds were formed. Today, examining a map, one can easily recognize these structures; there are over 600 hundred kettle ponds on the Cape. Some, like Salt Pond in Eastham were connected to the ocean and filled with salt water. Glacial erratics, or car size boulders which were dragged by the ice sheet and deposited in their present location, can be found scattered throughout the area. Rock Harbor gets its name from the large glacial erratic boulder found just north of the channel.

As the ice was melting, an outwash plain was formed from deposits that were carried by the water from the forward edge of the glacier. Sand, clay, silt, and gravel would be deposited to the south of the ice. If the melting were vigorous, a channel would be formed to carry the water and till. Bass River between Yarmouth and Dennis is an excellent example of this activity, as are a number of water basins on the southern side of Martha's Vineyard.

Shifting shoals of sand found along the coast, as can be seen on the satmap, are a product of the glacial history of the area. These areas are infamous for the shipwrecks that have occurred there since the time of the first explorers to the New World. Further out in the ocean, the glaciers also formed the plateaus that extend from New York City to as far north as Newfoundland in the Canadian Maritime Provinces. Better known as "The Banks," these rich, fertile fishing grounds lured early explorers from Europe to visit and reap the bounty of the ocean.

Even now, the Cape landscape is being changed and altered. Instead of a glacier, it is the slow constant changing of tides, wind, and storms that move the sand in a perpetual motion. Scraped from one location or eroded from dunes, the sand fills inlets, clogs harbors, and changes the coastline. On the outer beach, an average of three feet of dunes are lost every year. If the tide is high when a "northeaster" arrives with its hurricane strength winds, the destructive effect can be disastrous. Homes are washed away, new waterways produced, and a substantial altering of the environment occurs. These alterations offer us the opportunity to observe the forces of nature creating constant change on the face of Cape Cod.

This vertical view image, taken in the spring of 2000, shows Cape Cod and the Islands. The Elizabeth Islands are seen extending southwest from Woods Hole, the last island being Cuttyhunk. Martha's Vineyard and Nantucket are also visible in this cloud free view. The Cape Cod Canal can be seen as a thin waterway connecting Buzzards Bay and Cape Cod Bay. The light areas in the water are the constantly shifting sandy shoals that have been responsible for so many wrecks. In Cape Cod Bay, Billlingsgate shoal is easily seen on the west side of Wellfleet Harbor, as are the prominent Brewster tide flats. *Image courtesy NASA/JPL, MISR Team*

A closer look at the Islands: Cuttyhunk at the end of the chain extending from Woods Hole; Martha's Vineyard with Menemsha Pond and Aquinnah on the left and Chappaquiddick on the right; and Nantucket to the lower right. Other landmarks of interest are the New Bedford area at the top, far left, No Man's Island south of Gay Head at the southwest edge of Martha's Vineyard, and the tip of Monomoy Island north of Great Point in Nantucket. *Image courtesy NASA/JPL, MISR Team*

Human History of Cape Cod

As the glaciers receded and the land became habitable, Native Americans, who originally crossed over the land bridge that once connected Asia to North American, began their migrations south and east across the continent. As early as 12,500 to 10,000 years ago, Native Americans were present on Cape Cod, roaming the land, hunting, and gathering shellfish and fin fish. By the time the Pilgrims arrived in 1620, as many 75,000 Native Americans may have been present in New England. Early European visitors exploring the coastline would encounter natives who depended on the sea and coastline for sustenance. Many of Cape Cod's harbors and waterways had been used for generations.

Tales have been told of Vikings reaching the Cape and islands as early as 1000 A.D., but no evidence has been documented. Recent archeological excavations have found proof that the Vikings did have settlements in Labrador and may have been there as late as the 1300s. They probably explored and had villages in the Maritimes but did not extend their influence as far south as Cape Cod.

John Cabot, sailing from Bristol, England, reached North America in 1497 (probably New-foundland and the Grand Banks), describing a sea full of fishes. Looking for spices and gems in the New World, Cabot returned the following year for further exploration, but a storm destroyed the fleet, and only one vessel returned to tell of the tragedy.

Other nations, including Spain, France and Portugal, sent expeditions to explore the coast, establish outposts, and harvest the bounty of the sea. In 1602, Bartholomew Gosnold sailing with 32 crew, passengers, and intent on establishing a colony in what is now New England, first made landfall at Cape Elizabeth, Maine. On the 15th of May, he sailed into Provincetown Harbor. Cape Cod was first used as the name given to the area by Gosnold. Further exploration led to the discovery of Martha's Vineyard, which he supposedly named after his daughter. A small settlement was established on Cuttyhunk Island, but abandoned for a variety of reasons as the settlers returned to England. A memorial tower was erected on the 300th anniversary at the location of the first outpost. Gosnold is also remembered for his 1607 voyage that led to the settlement at Jamestown, Virginia, and the eventual colonization of the New World.

Samuel de Champlain, better known for his discoveries and mapping of New France, also explored Cape Cod in 1605 and 1606. Skirmishes with the Monomoyick Indians in Chatham prevented any chance of a settlement in the area. He also visited and mapped what is now Nauset Marsh. Captain John Smith, who had sailed with Gosnold and was the leader of Jamestown from 1607-1609, returned from England in 1614 to explore the coasts of Maine and Massachusetts. He named the area New England.

After the Pilgrims arrived in 1620, more ships arrived and the small Plymouth colony began to expand and settle in other areas, including Cape Cod. Contact with the Indians was usually peaceful, and the Europeans purchased land for their settlements. The Cape was settled starting with the Bourne/Sandwich area and slowly moving east. Over the years, agriculture and farming may have drawn the early settlers, but maritime activity increased and nearly every community would be involved. The harbors of Cape Cod would become important in the development of the communities.

Harbor Quiz

How well do you know the harbors and waterways of Cape Cod?

Most people purchase a non-fiction book and expect to learn about the subject suggested by the title. They do not expect to be tested beforehand on the material included in the volume. True, this is a book about the harbors and waterways of Cape Cod and the Islands, but it also contains, first, a series of images and clues to some of the most popular waterfronts found in the area.

Try your luck or skill at identifying these places.

If you get more than 16 correct, consider yourself a Captain and fit to sail the Cape. 11 to 15 qualifies you as First Mate. Anything below 10, you had better have some navigational help or stay on land. Answers are found throughout the book with the towns discussed, but if you want to peek, they are listed on page 224. Most images in the quiz were photographed from land in an easily accessible location. The postcard is over 100 years old, and the same spot that I used is still used today to produce picturesque images. I have no access to an airplane, so the aerial was shot from a helicopter. In addition, there are no quiz images of Martha's Vineyard or Nantucket. Good luck and smooth sailing.

1. In 1602, Bartholomew Gosnold landed here; in 1620, the Pilgrims spent five weeks here.

2. Some of the most famous marine research facilities and scientific institutions are found here.

3. Eat supper on this busiest of the south coast's harbors.

4. Largest outwash glacial stream on the Mid-Cape

5. A little tougher, a kettle pond off Pleasant Bay in Orleans, famous for its sailboats.

6. No water, must be bayside, but where? Extra clue: the creek forms a boundary between the same two towns as #4 does.

7. & 8. Two different ponds with the same name. What are the ponds called, and what lower Cape towns are they in?

9. Named for its famous alewife fishery, what is the name of this river that runs into Nantucket Sound?

10. Great place to watch the sun go down on Buzzards Bay.

11. Close to celebrated resort area with golf courses in Mashpee.

12. This river and harbor has Indian name; Corn Hill is on the far shore.

13. Over 100 years later, still a beautiful scene in Harwich.

14. A royal locale, the only harbor in Marstons Mills.

15. Famous for their bivalves on the outer cape

16. A "pleasant" place to sail.

18. A snug anchorage on the way to Chapoquoit Beach.

20. Connected to Pleasant Bay, this is almost like an Indian get together.

17. Gateway to the Cape.

19. Samuel de Champlain fought the Indians here in 1607 or as Shakespeare said, "All the world is a ………."

Cuttyhunk

Cuttyhunk is the last island in the chain of Elizabeth Islands that extend southwest from Woods Hole and collectively constitute the town of Gosnold. Cuttyhunk is the town seat of Gosnold, the smallest town in Massachusetts in terms of population. This last island in the chain is about 2-1/2 miles by 3/4 miles in size with a good, safe harbor that attracts sailors and cruisers during the busy summer season. Together with Martha's Vineyard and its adjacent island of Chappaquiddick, the island chain town of Gosnold is part of Dukes County

First discovered in 1602 by Bartholomew Gosnold who remained on the island for 22 days before returning to England, Cuttyhunk was bought and sold over the years for its wood and excellent sheep grazing locations. For over 100 years at the height of the whaling trade, island pilots were famous for sailing ships into New Bedford and other ports. They would sit on Lookout Hill waiting for passing whalers. In 1864, several New York businessmen bought most of the island and formed the Cuttyhunk Fishing Club to fish for striped bass. The island is now mostly private with about thirty year-round residents, but in the summer the population swells as homeowners and visitors are attracted to this island with few vehicles, no theater, no golf course, a gift shop or two, and one market. Visitors to the island enjoy fishing, sailing, kayaking, beachcombing, bird watching, and other activities in this quiet haven. A ferry brings tourists on a daily basis in the summer to visit, walk around, and enjoy the island.

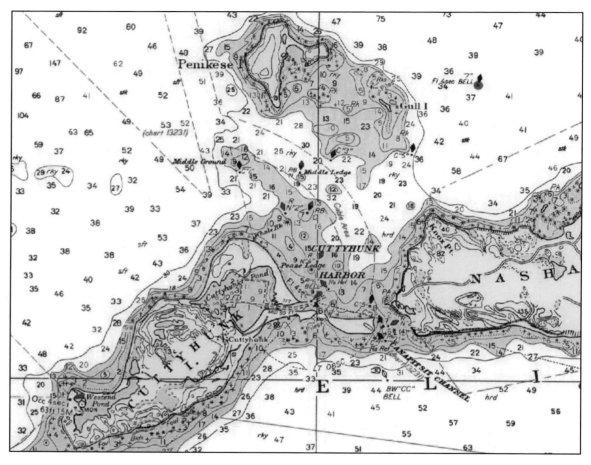

This chart of Cuttyhunk shows the island with its large, safe harbor and moorings in Cuttyhunk Pond. Two neighbors, Penikese to the north and Nashawena are two other islands in the Elizabeth chain. *Courtesy of NOAA.*

CUTTYHUNK MARINA
LONGITUDE   070°55.69
LATITUDE   041°25.69
Town of Gosnold

Once you dock at Cuttyhunk, you know your exact position.

Just beyond the red buoy is the breakwater that protects mariners entering Cuttyhunk Pond.

The ferry dock and the Coast Guard Station await visitors to the island.

Now owned by the town, the Coast Guard station was built after the hurricane of 1938 and deactivated in 1964.

The dock also offers charter fishing services, ice cream, and food during the busy summer season.

Cuttyhunk Pond with some of the boats moored there.

A view of the Cuttyhunk Pond from the hill.

This view north from Lookout Hill shows the pond and Penikese Island in the distance.

Freshly caught shellfish are available to vessels moored in the harbor.

This view northeast shows Nashawena Island across the harbor. Martha's Vineyard is the land on the horizon.

This early 1900s postcard shows the Cuttyhunk Lighthouse built in 1823, and the Gosnold Monument built in 1903 to commemorate the 300th anniversary of Gosnold's landing.

The Cuttyhunk Fishing Club is now a bed and breakfast inn.

This is a present day view of Westend Pond with only the monument standing.

The one room schoolhouse was built in 1873 and provides for students in grades 1 through 8. Students then must attend high school on the mainland.

The Methodist Church, built in 1881, has a striped bass as its weathervane. Other denominations occasionally use the church.

After a cruise, a sailboat returns to Cuttyhunk Pond.

Provincetown

Provincetown Harbor has a four hundred year history, starting with the first recorded visit by Bartholomew Gosnold in May of 1602. Eighteen years later the most famous visitors, the Pilgrims, sailed into the harbor on the Mayflower in November 1620. Part of Truro until 1714, Provincetown was incorporated in 1727. Most of the land was owned by the government and known as the Province Lands. At the outbreak of the American Revolution, its population was 250. The town had no roads, as all the houses faced the harbor, and going from one dwelling to the next involved simply walking along the beach or using a boat at high tide. For most of the nineteenth century, the maritime industry was the principal activity, with whalers, schooners, and a variety of vessels in the pursuit of whales and fish visiting the harbor. As late as the early twentieth century, there were seven large fish freezing plants and several fish curing and canning plants. The harbor was crowded with the whalers and fishing boats that supplied the plants. As the fishing industry declined, the plants closed, and now fewer fishing boats can be found in the harbor.

Today, Provincetown Harbor is a large deep bowl that is 30 to 90 feet deep with no dredged channel. It is about 1 mile by 2 miles in size; the breakwater, built between 1970 and 1972, provides protection to the sailor and boater. Slips, marinas, and boatyards are available to the cruising visitor. Of all the harbors on Cape Cod, Provincetown offers the most amenities, including the shops and galleries on Commercial Street, numerous fine restaurants, and an assortment of nighttime activities to satisfy anyone.

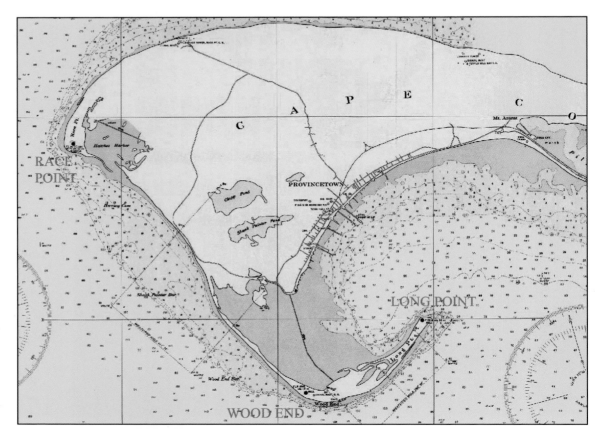

This early 1930s map shows Provincetown before the airport and breakwater were built and before the creation of the National Seashore. The three lighthouses, which are still active aids to navigation, guide mariners into the harbor. *Courtesy of NOAA.*

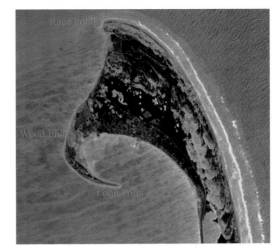

This NASA image illustrates how well protected Provincetown Harbor is from the Atlantic Ocean, where the surf constantly buffets the shore. (Courtesy of NASA.)

This aerial view of the inner harbor shows the two piers with Macmillan wharf on the right. The breakwater in the foreground was built to protect the inner harbor. The Pilgrim Monument is the distinctive tower in the center of the picture.

Race Point Lighthouse.

Wood End Lighthouse was originally built in 1872 and painted brown. The light was automated in 1961 and converted to solar power in 1981. It can be reached by walking across the breakwater from the end of Commercial Street.

Long Point Lighthouse.

This early 1900s postcard depicts what is now Pilgrim Park, the breakwater built in 1911 to prevent sand from entering the harbor, and Wood End light in the distance. Only the light and oil house remain standing.

This aerial view shows Long Point Lighthouse in the foreground with ships moving in and out of Provincetown Harbor.

Early morning fog partially obscures the Pilgrim Monument.

This view from the Pilgrim Monument
shows the two piers about 1920.

Early in the 1900s before the Pilgrim Monument was built in 1910, the town hall was the most distinctive building on the skyline. High Pole Hill would be the future site of the monument.

The ferry from Boston brought visitors to Provincetown. Notice the train tracks on the pier.

On a bright clear morning, fishing boats are moored at Macmillan Wharf.

A fishing boat tied up to the old fish dock.

The same scene almost 80 years ago. *Courtesy of the Library of Congress.*

Recreational vessels moored in the outer harbor.

The former Methodist church, now the town library, is a distinctive building along the waterfront.

Along the harbor shore looking towards the east end of town.

Buildings are boarded up and the town is quiet in the winter.

Dinghies and fishing boats tied up at the dock.

Two fisherman work the nets in this old image. *Courtesy of the Library of Congress.*

Before the sun has risen, fishermen are getting ready to head to sea.

Hauling a net with a load of fish in this old photo. *Courtesy of the Library of Congress.*

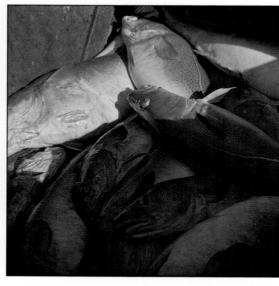

This catch of codfish was more common in times gone by.*Courtesy of the Library of Congress.*

A black backed gull sits on a trawler looking for a meal.

A fresh catch of bluefish on its way to market.

A brightly colored net on a trawler.

With the town hall steeple in the background, a variety of flags are available at this store on the waterfront.

A whale watch boat, now one of most common boats in the harbor.

Humpback whales are one of the species often seen on whale watching trips.

Distinctive tails called flukes are visible when whales dive.

Sunrise on a foggy morning finds a still and quiet harbor.

33

Gulls looking for a meal assemble around a boat returning from a fishing trip.

A schooner makes a stop in Provincetown Harbor during the summer.

Numerous dining opportunities are present along Commercial Street on the harbor.

Lobster buoys hang on a fish market on the harbor.

Some of the best bird watching opportunities are in harbors where the birds are accustomed to boats and people. This is a male eider.

Early morning in Provincetown harbor.

Pamet Harbor

Truro, at the wrist of the Cape, is a town bordered on the north by Provincetown, on the south by Wellfleet, on the east or backside by the Atlantic Ocean, and on the west by Cape Cod Bay. Pamet Harbor is located on the Cape Cod Bay side of the town and has a variety of small recreational and commercial boats. The Pamet River, which begins in the marshes behind Ballston Beach on the Atlantic side, meanders west for about three miles to its terminus at Pamet Harbor.

The name Pamet is derived from a tribe of the Nauset nation, Native Americans who lived further south in Eastham. The term "pamet" is also used by geologists to indicate a streambed covered with glacial drift. In mid November 1620, Myles Standish led an exploration of the area and discovered fresh water springs, animal traps, and stashes of corn. A prominent hill north of the harbor was named Corn Hill after this discovery. This corn would be used by the Pilgrims to plant the following spring in Plymouth. In return, the Pilgrims left behind trinkets as payment when they removed the corn.

On 16 July 1709, Pamet was incorporated and had its name changed to Truro. Many of the early residents were fisherman, and the town was prominent in the whaling industry. In 1720, Joshua Atwood was successful in his ability to harvest finback whales. As many as nine large whaling vessels hailed from Truro and sailed as far as the Falkland Islands. In 1874, over 1400 blackfish (actually pilot whales) were driven ashore on the bayside and yielded over twenty-seven thousand gallons of oil.

The first wharf was built in 1754, with others built in 1830 and 1837. During the heyday of Pamet Harbor between 1830 and 1855, more than fifty vessels could be seen moored at the docks. Over 500 men and more than 60 vessels were involved in cod and mackerel fishing that yielded tens of thousands barrels of fish. From 1837 to 1851, 15 schooners and brigs (schooners were usually smaller than brigs, which were 75 feet to 165 feet in length) were built at the mouth of the harbor. In the 1850s attempts were made to build a breakwater and wharf, but when difficulties arose, the project was abandoned. By 1870, the railroad had reached Wellfleet, and within two years, tracks had been built across Pamet Harbor and on to Provincetown. By the mid-1880s, the harbor was choked with sand and desolate. Even today, the harbor is difficult to navigate at low tide, and the county dredge is used to keep a channel open.

No longer able to use the harbor for large vessels, fishermen turned to weir or trap fishing. The first one was erected in 1881, and a total of six constructed by 1885. Including the circular pound at the end of the netting supported by poles and built at a cost of $8000 dollars, the weirs extended 2500 feet into deep water and required seven men to maintain them. Catches were sometimes extraordinary; in 1887 weir number 5 trapped forty tons of pollock in one day and also reported 300 barrels of mackerel at another time.

Today, Pamet harbor still poses problems for boats navigating at low tide, but at high tide the modern double launch ramp and the short run to the fishing grounds draws many fishermen to the harbor to launch their boats. Striped bass and bluefin tuna are the primary objective of many of these anglers. Few amenities are available to the boater.

Pamet harbor is usually quiet and peaceful and a great place to watch the sun go down.

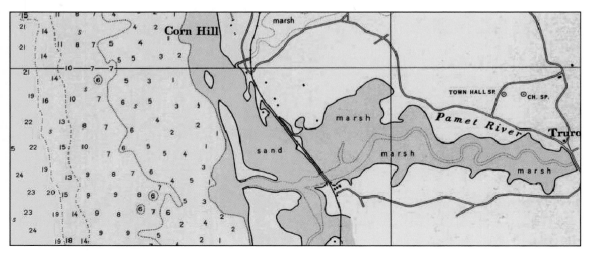

This 1934 chart shows Pamet Harbor with the railroad running north and south. Note how shallow the water is at different locations. *Courtesy of NOAA.*

This NASA view shows the Pamet River from the harbor, up the river towards the Atlantic Ocean on the right. The Cape at this point is only about 3 miles wide. The road in the center of the image is Route 6, which is the longest road in the United States.*Courtesy of NASA.*

An aerial view looking southeast shows the inlet at high tide.

A second aerial view illustrates the inner harbor with the launch ramp and the Pamet River on the left.

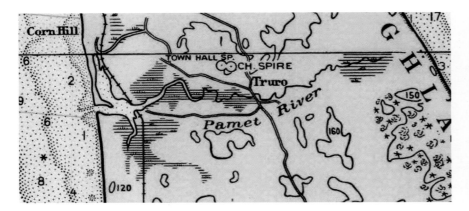

This 1975 chart shows the harbor as it is today. The railroad track has been removed from across the harbor; Corn Hill to the north is where the pilgrims discovered corn that had been stored by the Indians.

This view of the harbor is looking west out the inlet. Compare this to the first aerial view.

Fisher Beach is on the other side of the land in this view of Pamet harbor.

Dinghies line the shore to provide access to boats in deeper water.

Classic boats can be found in many Cape harbors.

Looking to the north side of the harbor and Corn Hill just beyond to the right.

Sunset at the town dock looking out the inlet.

A peaceful sunset in the harbor.

Pamet River before it enters the harbor.

Turkey vultures soaring over Truro are a common sight. The bald pink head distinguishes it as an adult.

Wellfleet

Wellfleet, in the middle of the Cape's forearm and about eight miles long, is bounded on the north by Truro, on the south by Eastham, on the east by the Atlantic Ocean and on the west by Cape Cod Bay. Originally part of Eastham and first called Billingsgate, the town was incorporated as Wellfleet in 1763. Similar in its history to Truro, whaling and fishing were successful commercial activities in Wellfleet. In 1776, British privateers blockaded the harbor and crippled the fishing industry. After the war, fishing became a prominent industry for the town. In 1802, five whalers weighing up to 100 tons sailed from Wellfleet. Smaller ships sailed and caught mackerel and cod. During the height of the fishing industry, numerous vessels were built along the shores of Duck Creek. By the 1850s, Wellfleet was only second to Gloucester in mackerel fishing with nearly 80 ships and over 850 men involved.

The oyster has also been a major product of the local flats and in the mid-1800s as many as 40 ships were supplying the Boston market with this delicacy. By the late 1800s, as many as 45,000 bushels of oyster seed was being planted in the Harbor. As fishing declined and the harbor became less navigable, fewer fishing ships could be found in the harbor, and by 1900, not a single schooner was sailing.

Today, Wellfleet Harbor supports a significant fleet of recreational boats in a variety of sizes. For the boater, there are many amenities with marine supplies and services, restaurants, and the town center only a short walk from the harbor. At the town dock, commercial vessels involved in the shellfish industry include trawlers, 30-40 ft. long,

that drag for sea clams and quahogs in the Bay outside the harbor. Smaller craft are used to harvest bay scallops and soft-shelled clams. But oysters are the primary shellfish product of Wellfleet. Many of the grant sites where oysters are cultivated can be walked or driven to. In mid-October, the town celebrates the oyster with its Oysterfest—a festival that involves oyster shucking contests, all varieties of bivalves available for consumption, an arts and crafts show, musical performances, and other activities involving the community.

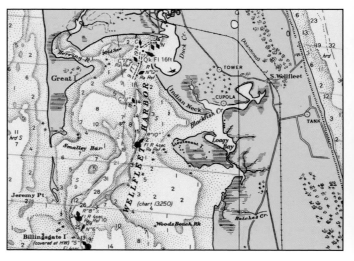

This more recent chart shows the changes that have taken place with Jeremy Point and the loss of land to erosion and storm action. You can use the two charts to identify the locations in the following images of Wellfleet. *Courtesy of NOAA.*

This 1950s chart shows the entrance to Wellfleet Harbor. Billingsgate Island, at the bottom left of the chart, just below the spit of land known as Jeremy Point, used to have a lighthouse and village, but is now covered at high tide with water. *Courtesy of NOAA.*

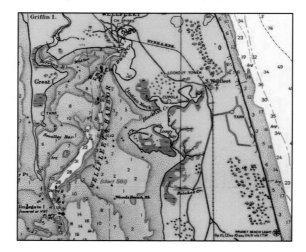

Looking south, Jeremy Point marks the end of Wellfleet Harbor.

The town pier provides protection for the boats moored in the slips.

This aerial view looking northeast shows the town dock and wide launch ramp in front of the Harbormaster's building.

An early 1900s postcard of Wellfleet Harbor.

Boats tied up on the protected side of the pier.

Buffleheads can be found in the harbor in winter.

Looking south across the town pier and the harbor, with Jeremy Point in the distance.

This old postcard shows Duck Creek
and Uncle Tim's bridge.

Duck Creek leads into Wellfleet Harbor.

Low tide at sunset with Great Island in the distance.

Chipman Cove is the mooring basin for many of the boats in the harbor.

Sunset with the town dock on the right.

As the sun is setting behind Great Island, a trawler returns to harbor while clammers are working the flats.

At low tide, some of the boats in the harbor are sitting on the flats.

Wellfleet is still famous for its oysters; grants are awarded to shell fisherman to grow and harvest oysters as seen here.

Next to the town dock, Mac's Seafood serves food and ice cream.

This late 1880's postcard shows the town of Wellfleet, Duck Creek, and the harbor beyond.

Pilot whales would be driven ashore for their oil. In 1885, a school of 1500 were trapped in Blackfish Creek and sold for $14,000.

Whether you prefer to sail or motor, an assortment of craft are available for rental.

Sailboats cruise the harbor in this old postcard scene.

Eiders are commonly seen in the harbor in the winter.

The state ship, *The Spirit of Massachusetts,* has visited Wellfleet Harbor.

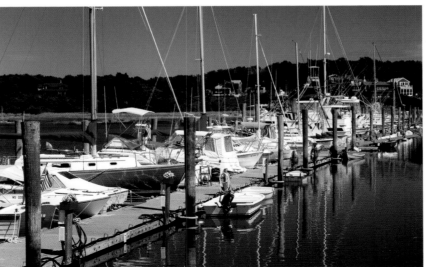

Boats moored in slips at sunset.

Looking west towards the end of the town pier.

Commercial boats at the town dock at sunrise.

Sunset over the inner pier with some of the smaller boats.

The final resting place for an old fishing boat.

Duck Creek with Uncle Tim's bridge in the background.

The Methodist Church strikes ship time with its bell. Uncle Tim's bridge is in the foreground

Commercial boats are hauled from the water and stored on the town.

Fishing boats are trapped in ice during the winter.

Eastham

In the early days, Eastham, which included parts of Orleans, Wellfleet, and Truro, was more involved in farming than the maritime industry and was famous for its turnips and asparagus. Even today, there are no deep-water harbors for boats. The north shore of Rock Harbor is mostly recreational craft. The mouth of Boat Meadow Creek provides some tidal moorings and has had a significant historical past. Early maps of Cape Cod show the river connected to Town Cove. In 1717, a whaleboat sailed up Boat Meadow Creek from the Bay to the Atlantic Ocean. A storm in 1770 closed the passage, and after a dike was built in the 1800s and the railroad bed was laid, there was no way to navigate from the Bay to the ocean.

On the Nauset Marsh side of Eastham, one of the earliest visitors was Samuel de Champlain who explored and charted the coast of Cape Cod in 1604-1607. At that time, large ships could enter and moor in what is now Nauset Marsh. Today small flat-bottomed boats can be found at Hemenway Landing that are able to navigate the marsh. At the National Seashore Visitor Center, Salt Pond, which is a good example of a kettle pond, is now used by the town for "put and take" quahogs for residents who have a clamming permit. It is also an excellent place for launching kayaks and canoes to explore Nauset Marsh.

Mid-tide along a bayside Eastham beach looking north towards Wellfleet and the dunes on Great Island. Several shallow water boats can be seen moored in the background.

Low tide on a bay beach.

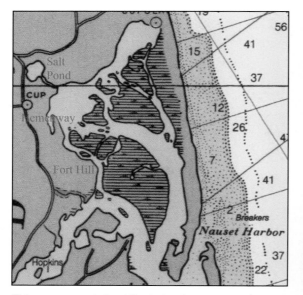

This more recent chart illustrates the constant changes that occur along the seashore in the location of the inlet. Salt Pond and Hemenway have a variety of small craft and launch ramps to provide access to Nauset Marsh. *Courtesy of NOAA.*

On a Bayside low tide the water may go out as far as half a mile.

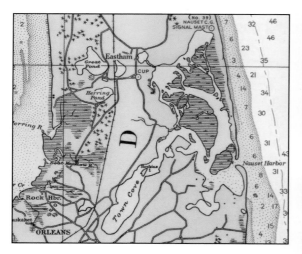

This 1950s chart shows most of Eastham and Nauset Marsh. Bayside is any of the beaches north of the Herring River. Boat Meadow River, located just above Rock Harbor, is a creek where shallow draft boats can be moored and protected from bad weather. The Eastham town boundary is the north side of Rock Harbor. *Courtesy of NOAA.*

An aerial view of the inlet with the constantly shifting channel that leads into town cove. In the center left is Fort Hill; the boats are moored at Hemenway Landing.

Early morn at Hemenway Landing.

Coast Guard beach, ranked as one of the ten best beaches in the United States, and the Coast Guard station, which was a former life saving station. The next image was taken just behind the station on a nature trail.

A great blue heron on a nest.

A great blue heron stalking through the marsh grass.

Nauset marsh at high tide at sunset looking towards Fort Hill.

Hemenway Landing

Dinghies and canoes are lined up at Hemenway Landing to be used on Nauset marsh.

Along the nature trail, a view of the marsh with the Coast Guard station in the distance.

A boat in Salt Pond.

Winter and the marsh is covered with snow.

This view from near the Coast Guard station is across the marsh.

Salt Pond is connected to Nauset marsh through a narrow channel. The building on the far side of the pond is the Cape Cod National Seashore Visitors Center.

An aerial view of Boat Meadow Creek with its winding channel that extends towards Town Cove.

At high tide, these sailboats are floating in deep water.

Another view of Boat Meadow at low tide shows the sand flats that extend out almost a half mile.
It doesn't seem possible that at one time whale boats used to sail into Town Cove from here.

The blue box in the marsh behind the creek
is used to trap greenhead flies.

At low tide, Boat Meadow is only navigable by shallow draft craft.

Orleans

Orleans was originally the South Parish of Eastham but became incorporated in 1797 after seeking independence. The maritime industry was an important influence in its early years, with salt works on both the bayside and Town Cove to provide for the needs of the fishing fleet. Depending on the supply of fish, small boats and fish weirs could be found plying their trade in local waters. Coastal whaling also thrived in the early years. Shell fishing has been an excellent economic activity and now with aquaculture techniques has become a stable industry.

Orleans is unique in that it has harbors on three different bodies of water: Rock Harbor, with its charter fishing fleet, is on Cape Cod Bay; Town Cove and Nauset Harbor connect to the Atlantic Ocean; and a series of ponds and rivers connect to Little Pleasant Bay.

Orleans — Rock Harbor

Raise your arm and Rock Harbor is on the inside crook of your elbow. The north side of Rock Harbor Creek is Eastham and the south side is Orleans. Historically, the harbor has been home to small flat-bottomed boats that would dig for clams and shellfish in the bay. It was also home to salt producers, who in 1814, refused to pay the tax demanded and successfully repulsed a landing party that tried to collect it.

The one limiting factor about the harbor is that it is tidal and for two hours before and two hours after low tide, most boats cannot leave or enter the harbor. Every spring dead trees are placed to mark the channel so that vessels can follow the deepest water. Even for its limitations, Rock Harbor is one of the prettiest and most active for its size, with the largest charter fishing fleet on the Cape. Trips for striper and bluefish are four hours and eight hours, based on the time of high tide. If you don't like to fish, stop by when the fleet returns to the harbor and see the day's catch as it is cleaned on the docks. Stop by at sunset during the summer to be entertained by a steel band as tourists and locals celebrate the end of another day. This is definitely one of the best places anywhere to watch the sun go down.

Two boats that drag for clams hail from Rock Harbor.

This aerial view shows the charter fleet at the bottom, the Eastham launch ramp and parking lot in the middle, and Boat Meadow Creek at the top. The rock, a glacial erratic in the water on the left side, gives the harbor its name.

A view of the harbor at high tide and the meandering creek and salt marsh. Some of the planted trees are visible just above the left breakwater.

This aerial view shows the glacial erratic and the entrance to the harbor. The inner harbor has to be occasionally dredged; the clean sand is dumped on the hill to the left.

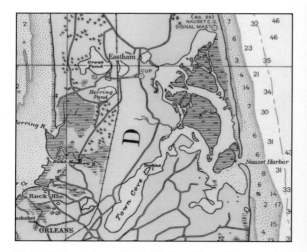

This old chart shows Rock Harbor, Town Cove, and Nauset harbor. *Courtesy of NOAA.*

The rock in Rock Harbor at low tide at sunset.

If you don't have reservations for a trip, stop by the charter service building to book your fishing outing.

Signs advertise the different charter boats.

Most of the charter boats can be seen in this image looking towards the harbor entrance.

Part of the charter fishing fleet at the dock

At sunset, the charter fleet with the narrow inlet in the distance.

Commercial boats at the dock with the Eastham shore in the background.

Cap't Cass is a local seafood restaurant.

Off-season and no boats; only gulls can be found in the harbor.

The Eastham side of the harbor has mostly small boats.

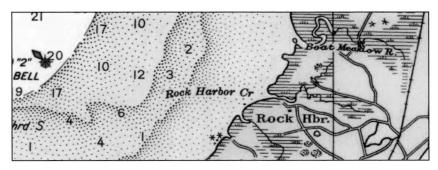

This chart of Rock Harbor shows the blue area that is part of the tide flats.

Young's Fish Market has been a fixture in Rock Harbor for many years.

Closed for the season.

Waiting for the water.

High tide and a serene view of the Rock Harbor channel.

The breakwater attracts people to celebrate the sunset.

Low tide and the trees that mark the channel are high and dry.

Waiting for the tide to get back into the harbor.

Town Cove

A mixture of craft are moored in Nauset Marsh at Nauset Heights.

This peaceful scene is Woods Cove, near Nauset Harbor

Lobster traps and lobster boats off Nauset Heights.

Mill Pond is a safe harbor close to Nauset Harbor.

Another view of Mill Pond.

71

Collins Landing is actually in Eastham, but has boats similar to those found at other landings on the cove.

Asa's Landing in Orleans is opposite Collins Landing, where the boats in the right background are moored.

A boat used to rake clams sits at anchor.

Some of the boats at the lower end of Town Cove.

The Orleans Yacht Club, among other activities, provides instruction for future sailors.

Kayaks are available for rental at a local marina on the cove.

Early morning, and sailboats are on the dock at the yacht club.

73

East Orleans

Meeting House Pond in East Orleans is the farthest extension of Pleasant Bay. From here, it is possible to reach the Atlantic Ocean in Chatham. Numerous coves and inlets can be found throughout the area and anybody interested in gunk holing will find hours of activity. Several picturesque ponds and coves are identified here. More wait the explorer who has the time to discover where the next creek will lead. Pleasant Bay is a spectacular body of water that provides numerous activities and enjoyment for a variety of boaters.

Dinghies at the town landing provide access to boats in the pond.

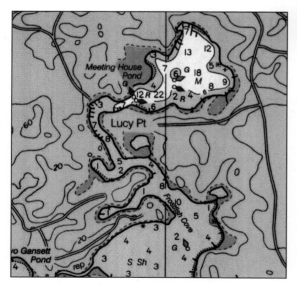

This chart of East Orleans shows Meetinghouse Pond and the River which connects to Little Pleasant Bay. *Courtesy of NOAA.*

An old boat half hidden in the grass.

The dock at the marina with large boats in the slips.

From the launch ramp, Meetinghouse Pond is quiet and undisturbed in the early morning.

A herring gull swims casually across the pond.

The dock at the marina.

At the dock, the outlet to the pond in the background.

Lucy Point along the River is across from this dock.

Along the River, boats are moored close to the homes.

Kescayogansett Pond, also known as Lonnie's Pond, is located along the River just south of Meetinghouse Pond.

Boathouses along the River provide winter storage.

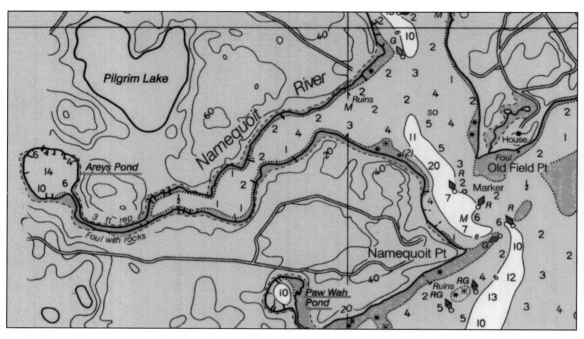

A chart of the lower end of the River displays two ponds that provide excellent safe moorings. *Courtesy of NOAA.*

Arey's Pond is home to more sailboats than any other type of craft.

A foggy morning, the beach roses are in bloom and the sailboats rest at their moorings.

Classic sailboats are common in Arey's Pond.

Almost the entire pond is captured in this view. The entrance for the pond is between the trees on the right.

Even at lowtide it is still possible to navigate around the pond.

Another chart shows the waterways and ponds in upper Little Pleasant Bay. (Courtesy of NOAA)

A boathouse looks out over Paw-Waw Pond.

A foggy morning at low tide at Paw Wah Pond, and the only one about is the great blue heron near the entrance to the pond.

PAH WAH POND
CONSERVATION
AREA

The pond leads into Little Pleasant Bay.

Belted Kingfisher

Quashnet Pond is another small body of water connected to Pleasant Bay, south of Paw Wah Pond.

Another view of Quashnet Pond

Pleasant Bay, Orleans

The Atlantic Ocean in the foreground, the dunes of Nauset Beach, and Pleasant Bay can be seen in this aerial image.

Late in the afternoon, near the launch ramp in South Orleans, Pleasant Bay is peaceful and calm.

The same viewpoint as the last image, but now the sun is just rising in the distance.

A willet hunts for food in the surf.

Boats moored in Pleasant Bay.

Chatham

Pleasant Bay

Chatham at the elbow of the Cape has the most shoreline of any town. It also has a storied maritime history. Pleasant Bay on the north and east sides of the town has many coves and waterways that connect to the Atlantic Ocean. In South Chatham, Stage Harbor, which connects to the Oyster River and Millpond, opens through a channel into Nantucket Sound, past the now inactive Stage Harbor Light. Stage Harbor was first visited in 1606 by Samuel de Champlain. After unfriendly relations with the Monomoyick Indians, he left the area, which was then settled by the English 50 years later. For the next 50 years, farmers were more common than fishermen, and the corn that the Indians had been growing for years was the town's principle crop. In the 1700s, fishing became more important and, along with Harwich and Barnstable, Chatham dominated the industry with catches of cod, mackerel, and halibut. The cod would be salted, and fast, seaworthy vessels would haul the fish south to the West Indies to trade for molasses and other products. Second only to the English Channel in ship traffic, the shores of Chatham were far more perilous, and even though lighthouses and life saving stations were built to assist the mariners, many traders met their demise in these dangerous waters. With the building of the Cape Cod Canal in the early 1900s, ships were able to avoid the treacherous waters off Chatham.

Today Chatham has waterways and harbors packed with boats used for recreational purposes as well as fishing vessels plying their trade in the near offshore waters. From the following images, you can see the diversity and abundance of craft that are found in Chatham.

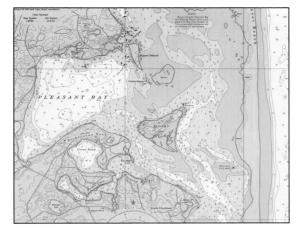

This chart gives you an sense of the Pleasant Bay region in Chatham. Several of the following images were taken in the cove at the left center region near Nickerson Neck. Images of Crow's Pond and Ryder's Cove can be found in the following pages. *Courtesy of NOAA.*

Muddy Creek forms the boundary line between the towns of Harwich and Chatham.

Looking across Muddy Creek into Pleasant Bay.

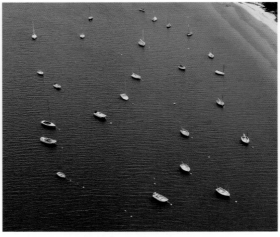

Mostly sailboats, these craft are anchored in the bay.

Muddy Creek to the right in this view of Pleasant Bay, Nickerson Neck, Eastward Ho golf course, and Crow's Pond, which opens into Chatham Harbor in the distance. Nauset Beach with its barrier beach dunes and the Atlantic Ocean can be seen in the distance.

Small craft moored near Muddy Creek.

Docks and moored boats in Crow's Pond.

A Ruddy Turnstone looking for lunch

A sanderling checks the shallows

Ryder's Cove

Looking southeast, this view of Ryder's Cove shows the marina and launch office in the top center.

Beyond the trees in the center of the image is where the previous aerial image was photographed.

Looking outward from Ryder's Cove towards Chatham Harbor.

Dinghies line the shore near the launch ramp. The odd-looking craft in the center is used to put in, move, and take out mushroom anchors used to secure the boats.

Kayaks along the shore in Ryder's Cove.

A great blue heron can be seen wading in the shallows

Chatham Harbor and
Aunt Lydia's Cove

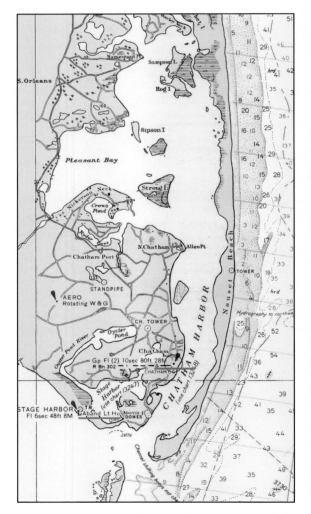

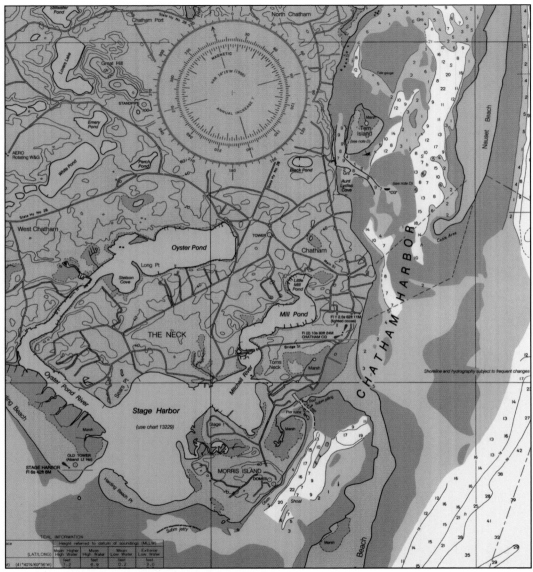

Compare these two nautical charts prepared for mariners more than twenty years apart and basically showing the same region of Chatham. As discussed earlier, the outer beach facing the Atlantic Ocean is constantly
changing; shifting sands can, in one storm, open or close channels, and produce hazards to navigation. It is
imperative that boaters obtain the latest information on local conditions. *Courtesy of NOAA.*

In the spring of 2007, a storm broke through the outer beach and formed this cut leading into Pleasant Bay. Strong Island in the center beyond the break provides a point of reference. Also, notice the shifting sand that alters channels, and opens and closes different bodies of water. These different circulation patterns can significantly alter the environment. In this case, ocean water is entering Pleasant Bay at a location closer to Little Pleasant Bay than to the original break across from the Chatham Lighthouse.

Chatham Fish Pier with the boats moored in Aunt Lydia's Cove.

The north view with Chatham Light in the foreground and Tern Island, which is next to Lydia's Cove, in the distance.

The Chatham Fish Pier on a foggy morning.

Some of the fishing vessels in Chatham Harbor.

The fish pier has a variety of gear to offload the catch.

Dogfish are hauled in, cleaned, iced down and shipped to market.

Boats swing on their moorings to face the flow of the tide.

A great black-backed gull looking for a free lunch.

Lighthouse Beach in front of the light. Notice the sand bar in the distance, which is also seen in one of the Outermost Harbor images.

Chatham Light, with its two distinctive beams, helps to guide mariners through the cut.

95

Millpond

This aerial view of Little Mill Pond shows the characteristic dock that can be seen in other images.

Dinghies and dock at Little Mill Pond.

A tranquil moment on the pond.

The dock on a foggy morning.

Another foggy morning view.

This panorama shows the number and variety of boats that use Mill Pond.

97

Oyster River and Pond

Looking up the Oyster River towards Oyster Pond

A string of buoys marks off the public bathing beach

Mostly sailboats moored in the river.

This old postcard shows fishing shacks along the river.

Wintertime along the river.

Stage Harbor

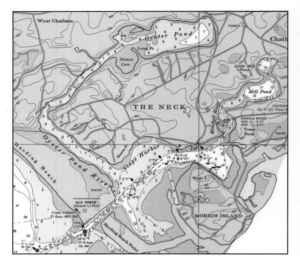

This 1970s chart, primarily of Stage Harbor, also shows the other waterways and anchoring areas discussed elsewhere in the Chatham section. Oyster Pond River leads to Oyster Pond, which is close to the center of town and has a public beach. The Mitchell River leads into Millpond.

An aerial view of Stage Harbor with its two piers; the left one is part of the yacht club, the one on the right for vessels that fish Nantucket Sound.

A string of boats in Stage Harbor on an incoming tide. These vessels are moored just to the right of the bridge in the center of the chart.

A cold winter day in Stage Harbor.

This view of Stage Harbor, taken just before an approaching storm, was shot from the causeway leading to Morris Island.

Stage Harbor Light was built to guide ships into the harbor, but when the canal was built it was no longer necessary.

An artistic approach to bottom painting.

Much of the area around Morris Island is protected as part of the National Wildlife Refuge system. These swallows flying across a nearby marsh are gathering for their migration south.

Sitting at the end of Harding's Beach, the light is now a private residence.

Outermost Harbor

A semi-palmated sandpiper explores the tidal flats.

This aerial view of Outermost Harbor, in the foreground, is just south of Chatham Light. Lighthouse Beach, seen in a previous image, is in the distance.

A greater yellow legs follows a lesser yellow legs across the flat.

A sanderling joins the party.

Boats with outboards to navigate the nearby waters are the primary craft found here.

Brewster

Brewster is the only town on the cape that does not have a harbor, but it probably has more sea captains' homes than any other community on the Cape. Bounded on the north by Cape Cod Bay, Brewster has one small creek that will have an occasional small boat moored in it. Paine's Creek is also a beach and an excellent place to launch kayaks.

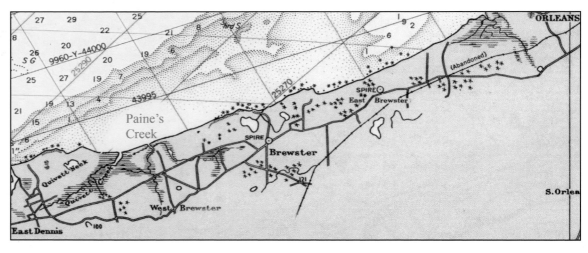

A chart of Brewster indicates the location of Paine's Creek. Notice the blue shaded area, which are the tide flats with no water at low tide. *Courtesy of NOAA.*

An aerial view at high tide shows Paine's Creek and the beach.

Low tide just in front of the beach with no water to swim or boat.

An approaching bayside storm.

Sunset at Paine's Creek.

A greater and lesser yellowlegs
stalking food along the shoreline.

Low tide in the middle of the creek.

Harwich

Harwich, like many of the other Cape towns, had its early economy based on agriculture and maritime endeavors. Over two hundred years ago, Harwich had as many as 20 ships fishing just off-shore for cod and mackerel. Another four or five boats were sailing to Newfoundland and Labrador for cod. By the mid-1800s, over 500 men and almost 50 ships were bringing thousands of tons of cod and mackerel into port. Herring were also sought after at the aptly known Herring River. Each family was allowed to keep two barrels of herring per year. Overfishing and harbors too small for larger ships resulted in a decline in the industry. Residents turned to growing cranberries, with the first bog planted near Pleasant Lake in 1847. Today, bogs can be found throughout the town.

Previous to 1883 there were no natural harbors along the south coast of Harwich. Today, Harwich's three harbors are busy with both recreational and commercial craft, with moorings and slips at a premium. It is not unusual to have your name on a waiting list and have to wait 10 to 15 years for a slip or mooring for your boat.

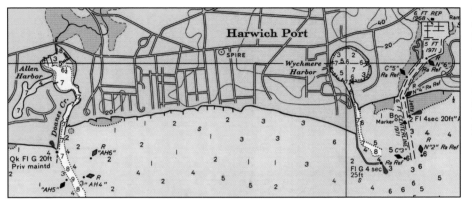

This 1950s chart shows why this community is known as "the town with three ports." From left to right, Allen Harbor, Wychmere Harbor, and Saquatucket Harbor provide anchorage for boats using Nantucket Sound and beyond. *Courtesy of NOAA.*

An aerial view shows the proximity between the two harbors with Wychmere on the left and Saquatucket on the right. Breakwaters allow a channel for the passage of vessels into both harbors.

The most western of the three ports, Allen Harbor has a deep water channel and a long protective breakwater against southwest winds.

107

Round Cove

Looking south into the channel that leads into Pleasant Bay. Round Cove is the only Harwich harbor on this body of water.

Two classic sailboats on a foggy morning.

From a lower elevation, Round Cove has a variety of small craft.

Even at low tide, boats are still floating.

A mute swan cruises in the harbor.

Saquatucket Harbor

Saquatucket Harbor, named for the local Indians who inhabited the area, is the largest municipal harbor on the south shore of the cape and the most recently built. Completed in 1969, the harbor was created from a small creek and a salt marsh to provide another anchorage for boats. With deep water and over 195 slips, it provides mariners easy access to Nantucket Sound.

This aerial view of the harbor with some of the slips also includes the harbormaster's office.

This perspective shows most of the slips, which are about 10 feet deep at low tide, and Nantucket Sound beyond. Monomoy Island can be seen in the distance.

Commercial craft in the harbor include a deep sea fishing boat and a ferry that makes trips to Nantucket as well as offering sunset cruises.

The Freedom Cruise Line provides services to Nantucket as well as seal/seabird cruises to Monomoy Island.

Male mallards are common in the harbor.

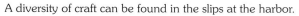
A diversity of craft can be found in the slips at the harbor.

Wychmere Harbor

Wychmere is the middle of the three harbors and is probably one of the most photographed locations on the Cape. Originally a salt pond with a small tidal creek, the harbor was not navigable until 1887, when 50 men with shovels dug a channel that allowed shallow drafted vessels to use the harbor. Exactly one mile around, a racetrack circled the pond, and before the channel was dug, sulky racing was held here for three years. The name, given by a group of businessmen who wanted to develop a resort, is based on the English "wich" for places with salt (Harwich and Sandwich) and "mere," Scottish for lake.

Wychmere Harbor is now a deep-water port with both recreational and commercial craft and a marine facility to provide services.

This aerial view of Wychmere shows the commercial dock in the bottom left and Nantucket Sound at the top.

Another aerial view shows the channel, the breakwater, and the additional boats at their moorings

Some of the commercial boats at the dock.

112

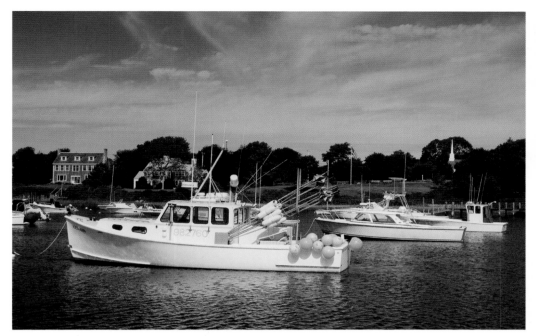

A typical fishing boat at a mooring.

On a quiet morning, a flotilla of craft float in the harbor.

The town maintains a building for commercial aquaculture projects.

A foggy morning and all is still.

Over a hundred years old, this postcard shows the photogenic harbor.

Another old postcard shows the classic sailboats that used to be found in the harbor over 100 years ago.

Ospreys, whose numbers were affected by DDT, can be found nesting in many of the Cape Cod harbors.

Sailboats float at anchorage in the harbor.

Pegasus ready to sail, and iced in.

Allen Harbor

Allen Harbor was originally known as Oyster Pond because of the Indians who used to camp here and harvest the shellfish, but when John Allen bought land on the harbor in 1756, the name was changed to Allen Harbor. After 1883, the harbor was improved so fishing vessels could enter and use the port. Vessels with too large a draft would have to anchor outside the inlet.

Now Allen Harbor has a yacht club, a marina to provide services, and a launch ramp that allows boats to gain access to Nantucket Sound.

An aerial view of the harbor shows most of the area, with the inlet at the top center. The yacht club is to the left.

Fishing gear on one of the commercial boats.

Some of the recreational vessels in their slips.

Allen Harbor with the yacht club to the left and the commercial vessels docked to the right.

The launch ramp and the channel to the inlet.

Herring River

The alewife or herring was an important natural resource for both Native Americans and early settlers, and in many towns provided important sustenance. In West Harwich, the now-named Herring River has been one of the most important herring runs on Cape Cod for over 300 years. Once a significant fishing industry in the early years, the alewife harvest is now town controlled with significant limits and restrictions.

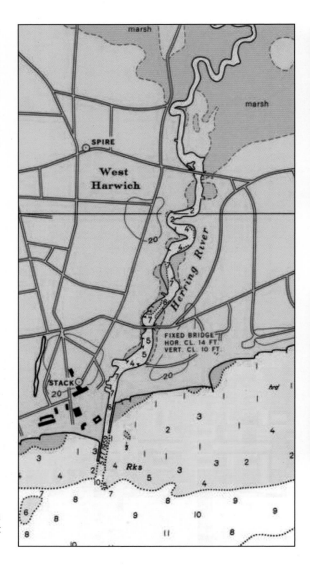

This chart shows the Herring River which meanders south from its source at West Reservoir. *Courtesy of NOAA.*

Compare this view with the chart and the following images.

This view of the river is just beyond the left breakwater, with a nearby launch ramp, just before the dock, that is maintained for Harwich fisherman.

Canada geese are common and breed throughout Cape Cod.

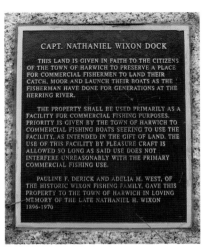

CAPT. NATHANIEL WIXON DOCK

THIS LAND IS GIVEN IN FAITH TO THE CITIZENS OF THE TOWN OF HARWICH TO PRESERVE A PLACE FOR COMMERCIAL FISHERMEN TO LAND THEIR CATCH, MOOR AND LAUNCH THEIR BOATS AS THE FISHERMAN HAVE DONE FOR GENERATIONS AT THE HERRING RIVER.

THE PROPERTY SHALL BE USED PRIMARILY AS A FACILITY FOR COMMERCIAL FISHING PURPOSES. PRIORITY IS GIVEN BY THE TOWN OF HARWICH TO COMMERCIAL FISHING BOATS SEEKING TO USE THE FACILITY, AS INTENDED IN THE GIFT OF LAND. THE USE OF THIS FACILITY BY PLEASURE CRAFT IS ALLOWED SO LONG AS SAID USE DOES NOT INTERFERE UNREASONABLY WITH THE PRIMARY COMMERCIAL FISHING USE.

PAULINE F. DERICK AND ADELIA M. WEST, OF THE HISTORIC WIXON FISHING FAMILY, GAVE THIS PROPERTY TO THE TOWN OF HARWICH IN LOVING MEMORY OF THE LATE NATHANIEL H. WIXON 1896-1970

This image was taken from the first bridge looking south. You can recognize the same house from the previous image on the east side of the river.

Taken from the second bridge, this image looks south towards the sound.

A mature black-crowned night heron roosts in the upper area of the river.

An immature black-crowned night heron.

A heron waits for its dinner in a dense thicket.

Dennis and Sesuit

Sesuit Harbor

Dennis is located between Brewster and Harwich on the east and Yarmouth on the west. Like Yarmouth and Barnstable, Dennis borders Cape Cod Bay on the north and Nantucket Sound on the south. It has noteworthy harbors on both coasts with numerous diverse vessels using the waterways. The history of Dennis includes significant events and activities associated with the maritime industry. Sesuit Harbor was the only harbor on Cape Cod where clipper ships were ever built. In the middle of the 19th century Bass River was a hub of maritime activity with an extensive fleet of coastal packets. Unlike many Cape towns that were named for locations in England, Dennis was named for the Yarmouthport pastor, Reverend Josiah Dennis.

Sesuit Harbor in Dennis on the bayside is about halfway between Rock Harbor in Orleans to the east and Barnstable Harbor to the west. A deep-water port that is navigable at all times, Sesuit has a considerable number of recreational craft.

Historically, as early as 1776, the area had salt vats that evaporated water to produce salt that could be used to process fish. Ships were built in several locations in the town, including the Bass River, but the noted Shivericks, Asa and his three sons, had their shipyard near the mouth of Sesuit Creek. Asa launched his first schooner in 1815, to be followed by a square-rigged brig, more schooners, and, eventually, eight clipper ships (over 1000 tons each) that sailed the world. The Shivericks built ships until at least 1862.

Today the harbor has a yacht club and three marinas to provide docking for boats. In addition to mostly recreational craft, several charter fishing boats and commercial vessels can be found in the harbor. As in other harbors, slips are at a premium and waiting lists exist.

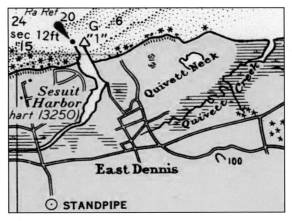

This chart shows the location and size of Sesuit Harbor. *Courtesy of NOAA.*

Northside Marina with the inlet on the right.

121

An aerial view of the major part of Sesuit Harbor.

A view of some of the boats in the slips and on the boat storage racks in the background.

The gas dock and café on Sesuit Harbor.

Since shifting sand is a constant problem in many of the Cape's harbors, the county maintains a dredge to keep the channels open. The deposited sand to the left of the breakwater will turn white and add to the beach.

The public launch ramp on the left bank of the channel.

The west side of the harbor looking towards the launch ramp.

Swan River

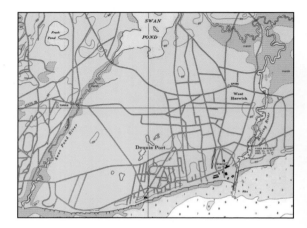

Much like the Herring River to the east, Swan River meanders for almost two miles from Swan Pond before it reaches Nantucket Sound.

Only small craft are able to navigate the upper section of the river.

Mute swans can be found in the upper parts

124

Sailboats ready for action near the mouth of the river.

In this aerial view of the Swan River inlet the sailboats from a previous image can be seen on the left bank.

The mouth of the Swan River looking east.

Bass River

The Bass River marks the boundary between Dennis on the east and Yarmouth on the west. Both sides have marinas, docks, and town landings that serve both pleasure and commercial boats. Geologically, the Bass River is an outwash stream created by the glacier when it melted over 10,000 years ago. Examine a map and you will notice that most of the streams in the mid-cape region run from north to south because this is the direction that the water flowed as the ice melted. The terminal moraine has become the highest elevations running along the central area of the Cape. Today, the Bass River is a busy waterway from its headwaters at Follins Pond to the mouth on Nantucket Sound. A variety of vessels can be found along its course.

Follins Pond is the headwater of the Bass River.

The only boats at Mayfair Boat Yard on Kelley's Bay are those that can fit under fairly low bridges in order to reach the sound.

Quiet coves and inlets can be found along the upper part of the river.

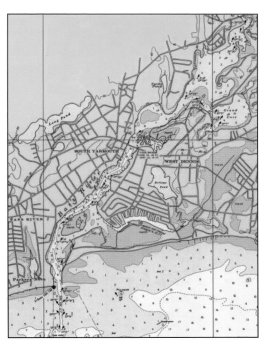

This chart shows the Bass River with Dennis on the right shore and Yarmouth on the left shore.

This launch ramp in Dennis allows boaters to access the river.

127

Early morning with the Route 28 bridge in the background.

A postcard over 100 years old showing the same
bridge, on which tolls used to be collected.

An aerial view of the river looking north with the same Route 28 bridge in the background.

Just above the Route 28 bridge, the Bass River Marina provides services and slips to boaters.

A Bass River dock looking south towards the sound.

Below the bridge large vessels have easy access to the channel.

The mill overlooks the river and West Dennis Beach in the background.

On the Yarmouth shore is the Judah Baker Windmill, which was built in 1791 and moved to its present location in 1866. Open seasonally, the mill was restored to its original condition in 1999.

The Dennis shore in the early morning.

Three sailboats floating in the river.

An aerial view shows the inlet and
Bass River Beach on the left.

West Dennis Yacht Club

This side channel off the Bass River leads to the West Dennis Yacht Club in the distance. The ever-popular West Dennis beach on Nantucket Sound is to the right.

Blue crabs are commonly found in Weir Creek next to the yacht club.

Some of the boats in slips at the yacht club.

Yarmouth

Like its neighbors to the east, Dennis, and the west, Barnstable, Yarmouth extends from Cape Cod Bay to Nantucket Sound. It also shares Chase Garden Creek and the Bass River with Dennis. Yarmouth has three villages, West Yarmouth and Yarmouth Port on the north shore along route 6A, and South Yarmouth along the shores of the Bass River. In the early 1800s, Bass Hole, on the north shore, was a center of maritime activity with windmills, salt works, and small shipbuilding operations. It was not unusual for packets, one-masted sailboats, from neighboring towns to race to Boston to deliver their product, with winners having bragging rights for their ships and sailing abilities. On the south coast, the Bass River also had salt works with windmills, shipbuilding, and similar enterprises. At times, over 150 vessels that traded goods from Maine to Carolina could be found in the river. With the changing of harbor conditions and the arrival of the railroad in the 1850s, maritime activity decreased.

Now, the north shore has minimal boating activities, while the Bass River has many marinas and docks with an assortment of vessels both commercial and recreational.

Chase Garden Creek, Grey's Beach

The boardwalk leads to the Bay while the railings to the right lead to the dock.

This harbor scene at low tide illustrates how the sand has filled the channel and limited the size of boats the can use it. The dunes to the right across the creek are Dennis; Sandy Neck can be seen in the distance to the left of the fence.

The northern boundary on Cape Cod Bay between Yarmouth and Dennis consists of Chase Garden Creek and Bass Hole, seen here at almost high tide. The boardwalk and the small dock are visible in this image. When the creek began to silt-in and sand prevented use of the harbor, what used to be a maritime center was moved further west

A small flock of sandpipers takes advantage of the receding wave to search for food.

Parker's River

This view of the Parker's River in South Yarmouth was taken just south of Route 28. A yacht club is found near the decorative lighthouse.

The tricolored heron is a rare visitor to Cape.

134

PARKERS RIVER

North of route 28, Parker's River meanders through a series of tidal salt marshes on its way to Nantucket Sound.

Two images that show the Parker's River inlet. Popular beaches are found on both sides of the waterway.

These two views of the river show the yacht club and the channel that is navigable at low tide and leads to the Sound.

Lewis Bay

Point Gammon Lighthouse in Yarmouth was used to guide mariners into Lewis Bay.

These two old postcards offer views of Lewis Bay as it was over 100 years ago.

Lewis Bay, as seen in this aerial view, extends to the left and becomes Hyannis Harbor.

Lewis Bay from Englewood Beach.

More lands are being preserved through land trusts; this park leads to a small cove off Lewis Bay.

Barnstable

Barnstable is the largest town on Cape Cod, both in size and in population. Located nearly in the middle of the cape, it is bordered by Yarmouth on the east and Sandwich and Mashpee on the west. The county is also Barnstable, and the offices are found on the north shore, just east of the harbor. The town has seven villages: Barnstable, Centerville, Cotuit, Hyannis, Marstons Mills, Osterville, and West Barnstable. Of those, Barnstable Harbor on Cape Cod Bay and Hyannis Harbor on Nantucket Sound are the two busiest ports in town. Osterville and Cotuit also have active harbors with numerous vessels of various descriptions. The smallest harbor and town marina is found in Marstons Mills. Like other towns on the Cape, Barnstable was an agricultural community in the beginning and then turned to the sea to harvest its bounty. Initially, large numbers of salt works could be found throughout the town. By the mid 1700s, the maritime centers were Lewis Bay and Hyannis Harbor on the south coast and Barnstable Harbor on Cape Cod Bay. Cotuit and Osterville were famous for their oysters that were delivered to market. Centerville was also involved in shipbuilding. The first lighthouse in Barnstable Harbor was built in 1826, and a Custom House was erected in 1855 to register all ships loading or unloading their cargo. At one time as many as 800 ships hailed from Barnstable. By 1854, the railroad reached Hyannis, and schooners that used to haul cargo to Boston and elsewhere were no longer in as much demand. The trains also opened the Cape to tourism as people could now visit using reliable and relatively speedy transportation. Among the early vacationers were President Ulysses S. Grant, who visited in 1874, to be followed a few years later by President Grover Cleveland. In the early 1960s President John F. Kennedy used to vacation at the family compound in Hyannisport. An accomplished sailor, he pursued the hobby on Nantucket Sound.

Barnstable today is the hub of the Cape, with tourism the primary industry. Its harbors are filled with more recreational craft than commercial vessels. Hyannis is still busy with ferries that commute to the islands, commercial fishing vessels that harvest a variety of fish and shellfish from Nantucket Sound, and other vessels to serve the public's needs.

An aerial view shows the narrow channel leading into the harbor. The beach to the left can be seen in other images.

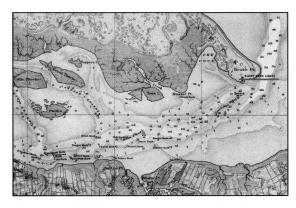

This chart of 1865 reveals the location of the lighthouse and the channel that leads into the harbor at the bottom center. *Courtesy of NOAA.*

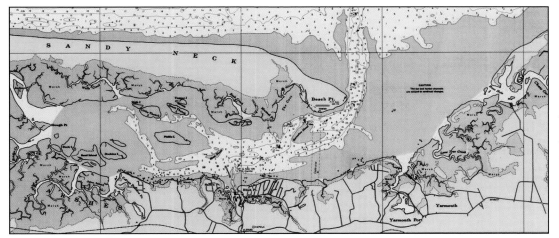

This more recent chart illustrates how the sand has built up on Sandy Neck; the lighthouse became no longer functional and was decommissioned in 1931.

139

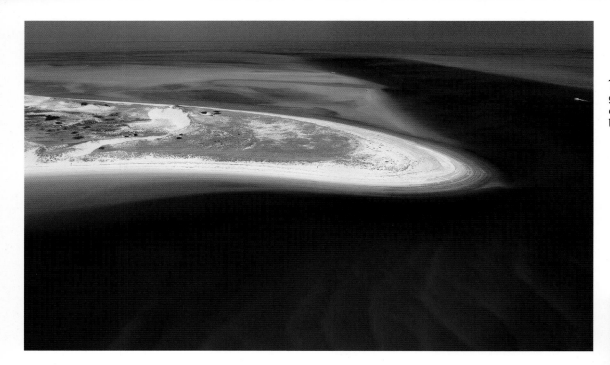

The tip of Sandy Neck has been continuously growing and extending further to the east. You can also see the sandbar to the north, as a solitary boat is heading out into the Bay.

Another shot of the harbor with a restaurant on the left and a marine store on the right.

A scene in the inner harbor with small recreational craft and the whale watch boat in the background.

This present day view shows the light on Sandy Neck.

Low tide at the beach. Sandy Neck can be seen in the distance across Barnstable Harbor.

Looking out the harbor, the whale watch boat is the largest vessel.

Another aerial view shows the boats in the slips with Sandy Neck in the background. As the picture was shot close to high tide, the harbor beyond is filled with water.

142

High tide looking out over
Barnstable Harbor.

A view across the harbor with Sandy
Neck Light the tower on the far right.

Sandy Neck Light still stands and is in the
process of being restored.

143

Hyannis Harbor

This early morning view of Hyannis harbor includes Great Point, and the ferry to Nantucket.

An aerial view of the harbor includes the lighthouse and the ferry dock at the top.

144

Not an active aid to navigation, the lighthouse, which had been moved from the north shore of Massachusetts, is a distinctive landmark for boats entering and leaving the harbor.

Hyannis, the busiest harbor on the south side of the Cape, has a variety of vessels.

A view of the harbor with recreational craft in the marina.

The Kennedy compound in Hyannisport.

A postcard, over 100 years old, shows
the wharf in Hyannisport.

Another view of the former north shore lighthouse.

148

A ferry sits at the dock on this wintry day.

An old postcard view of the harbor with the moored sailboats.

Decorated whales can be found throughout the town.

Galleries can be found along the sides of Hyannis Harbor.

With a ferry heading out of the harbor, the pier and moored boats are the same location as the postcards.

Hyannis Harbor

Centerville River

The Centerville River is a wide channel that leads to Vineyard Sound.

Homes with docks and boats line the Centerville River.

At the town landing, dinghies are tied up to the dock and take owners to their boats.

Looking South, the Centerville River in the distance leads into East Bay.

Looking North, the Bumps River connects to the Centerville River.

151

Osterville

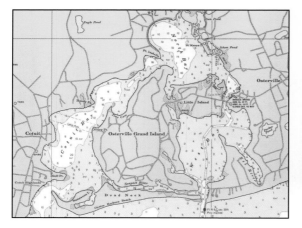

This chart shows the navigable waters in Osterville and Cotuit, including West Bay and North Bay. East Bay lies further to the right of this chart and Prince Cove is through the channel at the top of North Bay. (Courtesy of NOAA)

An older wooden boat rests in the water.

An early morning view of East Bay with the opening to the sound in the distance.

Many private homes have their own docks on the bay.

A classic sailboat at its mooring in East Bay.

Flowers bloom along East Bay

Dinghies are found near the town landing on East Bay.

West Bay has larger boats and marinas not found on East Bay.

Quiet waters on East Bay.

Reflections on West Bay.

West Bay with its large marinas in the background.

Looking north towards North Bay in Osterville.

West Bay, looking South.

Dinghies lined up at the town
landing on West Bay.

Prince Cove

Prince Cove is connected by the waterway to Osterville's North Bay but is the only harbor in Marstons Mills. If any one is interested in gunk holing, this is an excellent place to visit. It is also the town marina for Barnstable, and slips provide anchorage for small recreational craft.

More boats in slips, with the inlet to the cove through the trees.

This view from the launch ramp shows the end of the waterway.

Cotuit

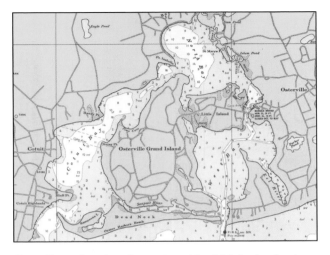

Cotuit Bay is found on the western side of this body of water.

Early morning sun on Cotuit Bay.

Two images of boats found on Cotuit Bay.

An early postcard of
the beach in Cotuit.

A launch ferries owners to their boats.

Beach roses bloom in spring on Cotuit Bay.

Cotuit Bay with the many boats moored there.

Town landing on Cotuit Bay

The Cotuit Rowing Club has several shells near the town landing.

Mashpee

Mashpee is located between Barnstable to the east, Falmouth to the west, and Sandwich to the north. With waters on Nantucket and Vineyard Sounds, there are numerous recreational craft, but there is no traditional town harbor. Several landings are available throughout the town where boats can be launched. In the early days, herring and oysters would be farmed from the sea. Beginning in the 17th century, Native Americans displaced from their ancestral lands were relocated to Mashpee, which at first was designated as a Plantation.

Today, Mashpee is a tourist destination known for its excellent beaches. It also has numerous Native American activities and cultural sights.

Located on Popponesset Bay, Mashpee Neck Marina is a full service marina for the local boater.

Some of the slips at the marina.

After a day on the water, there are places to relax.

Salty Dog waiting for a ride in a dinghy on Ockway Bay.

PIRATES COVE
BOAT RAMP

RECONSTRUCTED
1987

TOWN OF MASHPEE
PUBLIC WORKS DEPT.

The launch ramp allows boaters access to Popponesset Bay.

Ockway Bay, Mashpee.

Falmouth

Falmouth, situated at the southwest corner of Cape Cod, is its second largest town, with over 68 miles of shoreline, including creeks, waterways, harbors, and beautiful beaches. On the south, Falmouth borders Vineyard Sound, and on the west Buzzards Bay. Beginning at Waquoit Bay, which is the boundary with Mashpee, harbors and anchorages in Falmouth include Eel Pond; Bourne's Pond; Green Pond; Great Pond; Falmouth Harbor; Woods Hole, comprised of Little Harbor, Great Harbor, and Eel Pond; Quissett; West Falmouth; Wild Harbor; and Megansett Harbor in North Falmouth. In addition, there are numerous inlets and creeks where boats can be found.

There are seven villages that constitute Falmouth: Falmouth, East Falmouth, North Falmouth, Silver Beach, Teaticket, Waquoit, and Woods Hole. Agriculture and farming were the first industries, but the sea had its lure and by the 1800s maritime activities could be found throughout the town. Falmouth had its own fleet of packet ships that carried on trade along the coast. Salt works were found in most areas of the town, with windmills present to pump water into evaporating vats. In New York, a bushel of salt could be sold for a dollar, and a Captain might make as much as $100 on a single trip. Shipbuilding was established in good numbers in the different harbors, but Woods Hole was the most important because it built not only coastal craft but whalers that sailed the Pacific and returned to port with thousands of barrels of whale oil and other products. The golden age of whaling ended in the 1860s and with it the industries that supported it.

Today, Falmouth is a tourist destination with thousands of visitors, some that take the ferries to the islands, and others in the resorts throughout the town. The harbors are packed with boats of all description, moorings are at a premium, and launch ramps are busy with day-trippers. Yacht clubs and marinas can be found throughout the town on the various waterways. Woods Hole is now famous for its three scientific institutions that include the Marine Biological Laboratory, Woods Hole Oceanographic Institute, and NOAA, The National Marine Fisheries Services.

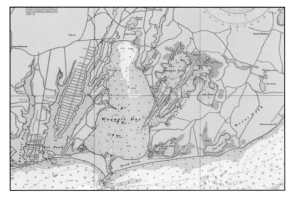

A modern chart shows the waters east of Falmouth Harbor, including Waquoit Bay, Eel Pond, and Bourne's Pond. East Falmouth includes several communities, but for discussion in this book the term relates to the waters between Mashpee and Falmouth Harbor. *Courtesy of NOAA.*

A sand spit on Washburn Island in Waquoit Bay.

Managed by the Massachusetts Department of Conservation and Recreation and NOAA, the estuarine research reserve includes 3,000 acres of open waters, barrier beaches, marshlands, and uplands. Besides providing long-term protection to the area, continuing research advances our knowledge and understanding of the different habitats.

The most northern part of Waquoit Bay has many boats at moorings.

Numerous shorebirds, like this sanderling, can be found in the bay.

Near the town landing on Waquoit Bay.

An aerial view of Eel Pond and its inlet. Washburn Island is to the left.

These boats are tied up just North of the bridge seen in the previous aerial.

Green Pond.

Boats tied up at the marina on Child's River, which connects to Eel Pond.

Dinghies on the shore of Green Pond.

A semipalmated plover wanders along the shore in search of food.

Great Pond.

Beach roses bloom near the inlet.

Falmouth Harbor

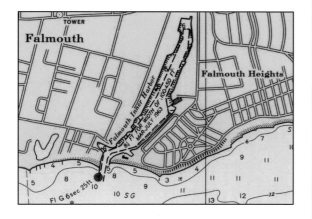

Compare the chart and the aerial image of Falmouth Harbor. The harbor itself is much smaller than the bodies of water to the East, but is more active with ferries to the Islands, commercial craft, and several marinas and boatyards. *Chart, courtesy of NOAA.*

The east side of the harbor with its large vessels and boatyards.

On the western side of the harbor, this sailboat is for hire; the ferry boat behind it makes trips between Falmouth and Oak Bluffs.

Falmouth Harbor, looking North from the yacht club.

Large sailboats tied up at the marina docks.

Looking South towards Vineyard Sound, with Martha's Vineyard in the distance.

With a lack of available mooring space, small craft are stacked in racks on the side of the harbor.

An immature herring gull can be identified by its mottled feathers. After three years, the gull reaches maturity.

A ring-billed gull sits on a post in the harbor.

Woods Hole

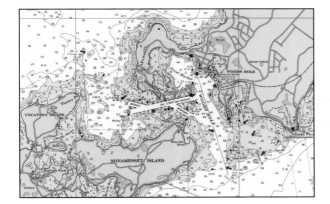

Several distinctive anchorages can be seen on this chart of Woods Hole. Little Harbor, just below the name Woods Hole, has been the site of government agencies for over 150 years, and now has an active Coast Guard Station. Great Harbor is a hectic, active harbor with research vessels, ferries, and commercial fishing boats, as well as a yacht club with recreational craft. Eel Pond provides moorings in a protected anchorage locale. Across the channel between Uncatena and Nonamesset, Hadley Harbor is a quiet body of water. It also should be noted that Woods Hole Passage is considered one of the ten most dangerous channels in the world. It is not unusual to find unfamiliar navigators on the rocks. Underlined in red, Nobska Lighthouse looks out on Vineyard Sound. *Courtesy of NOAA.*

Visitors to Woods Hole have numerous places to see and explore.

An aerial view of the area shows Juniper Point, with Little Harbor on the right and Great Harbor to the left. Buzzards Bay is in the background with the south coast of Massachusetts on the horizon.

Another aerial view shows Great Harbor, Juniper Point, and Martha's Vineyard across Vineyard Sound.

169

An active aid to navigation, Nobska Point Lighthouse looks over Vineyard Sound.
The keeper's house is still used by the Coast Guard for housing.

Early morning light in Little Harbor.

Little Harbor and the Coast Guard Station.

A stereo view of Little Harbor more than 130 years ago.

This postcard of Little Harbor over 100 years ago shows the buoy dock and a vessel that may have been a lightship.

The aquarium, a major attraction in town, has displays and animals from the area. It is a great facility to see fish and other organisms in their natural habitat.

The other side of Little Harbor had large homes as seen in this old postcard from the same era.

Another old postcard encompasses Little Harbor looking out into the sound.

The rear of the Woods Hole Oceanographic Institution with its research vessels and docks.

An old postcard shows Great Harbor in Woods Hole.

Another old postcard of Great Harbor with Penzance Point in the background.

Penzance Point, as in this old postcard, has many large homes.

Over 100 years ago, the docks in Woods Hole were busy with activity. The original fisheries building stands in the center.

172

Eel Pond, looking towards the Marine Biological Laboratory, which consists of the brick buildings in the background.

A sailboat rests on a foggy morning in Eel Pond.

The Marine Biological dock in the winter, with a vessel used to collect specimens.

Eel Pond on a quiet summer morning with the MBL on the right and with WHOI in the center.

On a winter's morning, no specimen collecting today.

Before sunrise, the dinghies and docks near the MBL.

174

Hadley Harbor: Tarpaulin Cove

Classic sailboats line the dock in Hadley Harbor, across from Woods Hole.

An aerial view of Hadley Harbor.

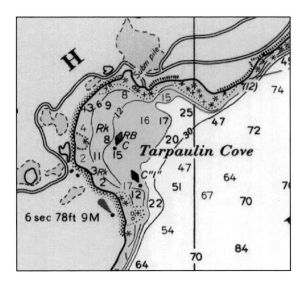

Further down Naushon Island is Tarpaulin Cove with its quiet protected waters and lighthouse. *Courtesy of NOAA.*

An aerial view of the cove looking southeast.

Tarpaulin Cove Lighthouse, with the cove in the background

Quissett Harbor

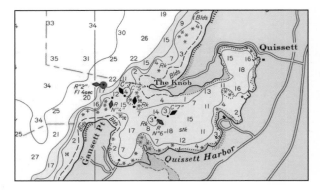

A modern chart shows the protected harbor of Quissett on the Buzzards Bay side of Falmouth. *Courtesy of NOAA.*

The shore of Buzzards Bay, Quissett Harbor, and Vineyard Sound in the distance.

An aerial view of the Gansett section of Quissett Harbor

Inner Quissett Harbor, with the house in the background that can also be seen in the previous aerial.

A postcard, over 100 years old, shows Quissett Harbor.

Iced in, Quissett Harbor in the winter.

Looking from the boatyard into the harbor.

The Knob, which can be seen on the chart, is a great place to see Buzzards Bay.

Looking across Quissett Harbor towards the boatyard.

West Falmouth

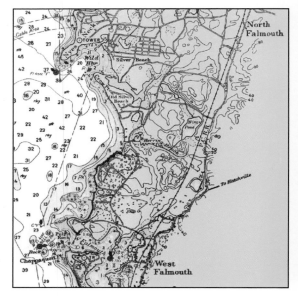

On this modern chart, West Falmouth is the protected harbor at the bottom, with Wild Harbor at the top. The popular Old Silver Beach is found just south of Wild Harbor. *Courtesy of NOAA.*

An aerial view of Snug Harbor in West Falmouth. A town landing can be seen in the top center. The dinghies to the left of the town pier can be seen in the next image.

Snug Harbor, West Falmouth.

An aerial view of an area within West Falmouth Harbor.

A picturesque boathouse in West Falmouth.

Looking west out of the harbor.

Unlike the outer Cape, which has harbors with mostly sandy bottoms, harbors along Buzzards Bay have a rocky surfaces.

A flag flies at the town pier in West Falmouth.

179

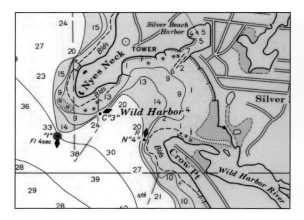

Wild Harbor

An aerial shot of Old Silver Beach.

Mallards rest along the harbor in winter.

Sailboats for rent on Old Silver Beach.

These two images are of the slips in Fiddler's Cove.

As you travel North along the Buzzards Bay coast, there are numerous coves and inlets. Some only have a few shallow drafted boats, while others have marinas and yacht clubs. This is Fiddler's Cove in North Falmouth with its narrow inlet.

North Falmouth

This hundred year old postcard
shows North Falmouth.

Megansett Harbor is the primary waterway in North Falmouth and this aerial view
shows the breakwater, the town landing and the yacht club. The water, Squeteague
Harbor, and the land to the top far left is part of the town of Bourne

This view is from a former resort hotel and is looking almost the opposite direction from the previous aerial. The Megansett Yacht Club
is the building to the right.

Tied up dinghys next to the harbor pier

Looking south along the coastline of North Falmouth.

This old postcard also shows the
North Falmouth shore.

With the hooked beak, the cormorant is able to catch fish.

With the beach and breakwater to the left, kayakers
find a safe place to paddle in the harbor.

Inner Megansett Harbor

Bourne

Bourne, part of Sandwich for over 200 years and the last settlement on the Cape to be incorporated, is the westernmost town and the gateway to the Cape. It is found on both sides of the Cape Cod Canal and includes both automobile bridges and the railroad bridge. There are eleven villages in Bourne; those with harbors include Buzzards Bay, Cataumet, Monument Beach, and Pocasset. Bourne's harbors are found on Buzzards Bay, as the town has no waterfront on Cape Cod Bay.

As early as 1622, Myles Standish expressed an interest in building a canal in place of the "Manaomet" (Monument River) River and Scusset River to connect Buzzards Bay and Cape Cod Bay. The Aptucxet Trading Post was constructed by the Pilgrims in 1627 near the mouth of the Manaomet River on Buzzards Bay to allow ships to trade goods with New York to the south without having to go around the Cape. In the early 1700s, Bourne's abundant supply of herring far exceeded its demand as a fish food, and the excess was used to fertilize the corn planted in the fields. Salt works were found throughout the town until the mid-1800s when salt was discovered in New York and could be mined inexpensively. By the 1800s ships were being built on the Back River near Monument Beach for coastal trading and the West India commerce route. Schooners, sloops, and barks were the typical vessels built.

Now, Bourne is a tourist destination with numerous harbors and waterways for the mariner. Also, the canal offers abundant activities with fishing, a nearby bike trail and several campgrounds in the vicinity.

Red Brook Harbor

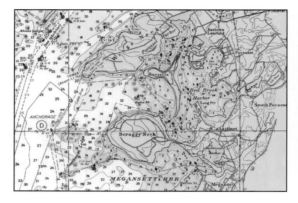

Reading the chart from bottom to top: Megansett Harbor is part of Falmouth; Red Brook Harbor, behind Bassett's Island, is in Bourne; and Pocasset is at the top. An inactive lighthouse is at the tip of Wing's Neck. The dotted parallel lines to the left are part of the channel that is the Cape Cod Canal. *Courtesy of NOAA*.

A view of the harbor from the "lighthouse."

An aerial view of Red Brook Harbor with the marina in the background.

Not a lighthouse, this building is a local real estate office.

Distinctive dinghies in the harbor at a dock.

The shoreline along the harbor.

Behind the marina, slips are packed with boats.

Pocasset

Scenes along the Pocasset River with numerous moored sailboats.

Along the Pocasset River with Bucky's Boatyard in the background.

Over 100 years old, these two postcards show views of the Pocasset River.

At the end of Wing's Neck is the lighthouse.

The lighthouse in winter.

Wing's Neck Lighthouse overlooks Buzzards Bay.

Monument Beach

Monument Beach.

An aerial view looking south in the Monument Beach area.

The office is painted with a local scene.

Monument Beach Marina in Phinney's Harbor.

Phinney's Harbor.

Cape Cod Canal

No survey of Cape Cod harbors would be complete without a discussion and images of the Cape Cod Canal. The first inspiration for a canal was probably Myles Standish's idea, in the early 1620s, to facilitate commerce between the Plymouth Colony and the Dutch in New York. With nearby rivers emptying into Buzzards Bay and Cape Cod Bay, the feasibility of a channel was possible, but the technology and engineering would not be available for 300 years. During the Revolutionary War, George Washington explored the viability of a canal to protect ships from enemies. The first survey was completed in 1776, and for the next 100 years more surveys were completed and several projects initiated but the overwhelming construction problems prevented any attempt to build a canal. By the end of the 19th century, with shipwrecks occurring at an average of one every two weeks, the demand for a canal became imperative

The first significant attempt at construction began in June 1909 with August Belmont as President of the Boston, Cape Cod, and New York Canal Company and William Parsons as Chief Engineer. By 1910, construction was full steam ahead, with the railroad bridge completed in September of that year. The two automobile bridges were completed in 1912 and the canal opened for traffic in July 1914. Unfortunately, the original canal had difficulties with its depth, originally 15 feet and by 1915, 20 feet, and its width of only 140 feet. When combined with the swift current this created severe navigational problems. In addition, the bridges, which spanned the canal, had to be

opened to allow marine traffic to pass. Accidents and canal closures diminished the success of the canal. During the First World War, the federal government took over the operation of the canal. After the war, Belmont resumed operations, but he tried to sell it back to the government. In 1928, Belmont finally succeeded, selling the canal for $11,500,000. The Army Corps of Engineers was directed to operate and improve the waterway.

Improvements to the canal included two fixed automobile bridges that were built starting in 1933 and opened to traffic in June 1935. The bridges were built on higher pieces of land to insure a maximum vertical clearance of 135 feet to allow ocean-going vessels to pass beneath them. Because of grade problems, the railroad bridge had to be located in the same original area and the Corps choose a vertical lift design. In the raised position, there is 136 feet of vertical clearance to allow ships to pass. It was also determined that the canal had to be widened and after conducting studies it was feasible to have a direct approach to the canal on the west end to prevent shoaling. In 1935 work commenced on a 480 feet wide channel, 32 feet deep, with a 17.4 mile channel that was completed in 1940. The two-way Cape Cod Canal is the widest sea level canal in the world. It has also received several prestigious awards including the National Historic Civil Engineering Landmark designated in 1985 and the Chief of Engineers Award of Excellence in 1986. The canal is an engineering marvel that was built to prevent shipwrecks and now provides safe passage to a significant number of vessels.

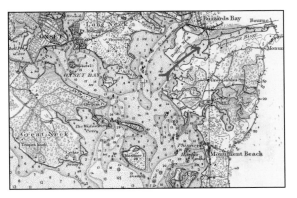

This chart, before the canal was built, shows the location of the river that would eventually become the canal. *Courtesy of NOAA.*

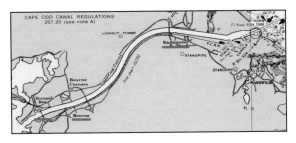

This modern chart shows the 7.8 miles of the land cut canal. The 3 bridges are underlined in red. *Courtesy of NOAA.*

Looking north, along the canal there are numerous rest and observation areas.

The east end of the canal opens into Cape Cod Bay. Just to the left of the Sandwich Power Station is the Sandwich Harbor.

A postcard from the early 1920s shows a ship passing through one of the road bridges. The narrow channel caused numerous problems to early marine traffic.

The Sagamore Bridge, nearest to the east end of the canal, is 1408 feet long with a horizontal clearance of 550 feet and a vertical clearance of 135 feet.

Looking west down the canal with the Herring Run Recreation Area just to the left of the road. On both sides of the canal are bike paths with several points of access.

Fishing is a favorite activity along the canal.

The Bourne Bridge is the same design as the Sagamore Bridge but is almost a thousand feet longer with the same vertical and horizontal clearances.

A cruise boat passes beneath the Bourne Bridge.

Fog rises from the canal on a cold winter morning underneath the Bourne Bridge.

The railroad bridge is at the west end of the canal.

This image shows the original railroad bridge completed in 1910. *Courtesy of Library of Congress.*

A sailboat has just passed under the railroad bridge.

A close-up of one of the towers.

Lowered, the bridge allows train to pass over the canal.

This aerial view of the west end of the canal has Taylor's Point Marina in the foreground, Massachusetts Maritime Academy at the top, and the Cape Cod Canal extending at the top left into the distance.

An old postcard shows the bridge in a lowered position.

Another view of Taylor's Point Marina with the railroad bridge in the background.

A park in Buzzards Bay abuts the bridge.

Ice floats through the canal during a cold winter stretch. With a 6 knot current and a change of tides, the canal is usually free of ice.

Tugs at the west end of the canal provide assistance, if necessary, to marine traffic.

The park and bridge in the winter.

Cleveland Ledge Lighthouse in Buzzards Bay provides an active aid to navigation for ships approaching the canal. Almost two miles from the nearest land and marking the south approach to the canal, this lighthouse is the only one named after a President.

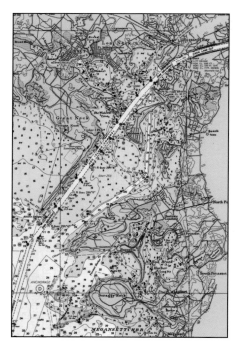

A chart of the west end of the canal showing some of the 9.6 miles of approaching channels. *Courtesy of NOAA.*

Sandwich

Sandwich, the oldest Cape Cod town, was settled in 1637 by residents of Saugus, who were given permission by the Pilgrims in Plymouth to locate a plantation here. With waterfront only on Cape Cod Bay and a nearly continuous sandy beach that stretches to Sandy Neck, Sandwich has no deep-water harbors on Cape Cod Bay. The shifting sands prevent creeks and inlets from being used as anchorages. An active deep-water harbor of refuge is found at the east end of the canal. It provides a safe, protective marina to recreational boats, as well as facilities where commercial vessels can off-load their catch.

In its early years, Sandwich also included what is now Bourne. Because of the availability of running water and an abundant supply of wood, it became a manufacturing center. Probably the most recognizable now were the glass factories, but the town produced other items, including railroad cars, tacks, and cotton textiles. Sandwich had an interesting whaling industry in the early years. Dead whales would float onto the Sandwich beaches of Cape Cod Bay because the early whalers were not very proficient in capturing dead or wounded whales. Men, delegated men from the town, would be responsible for seeing to the harvest and disposal of the whale.

Today, Sandwich's historic buildings, museums, and mill are an attraction for its visitors. Boaters are able to use Sandwich Harbor at the east end of the canal.

Several creeks empty into the bay in East Sandwich, but only shallow drafted vessels are able to navigate.

The boardwalk crosses Mill Creek and extends to the beach at Town Neck.

Also on the bayside, the channel between the breakwaters has filled in and moved to the east.

On the south side of the canal can be found the Sandwich Marina.

The Coast Guard maintains several vessels to aid navigators; the pilot boat ferries local qualified captains to ships who wish to use the canal; the fish plant in the background is falling into disrepair.

This old launch is now used as planter.

A fishing boat returns to the harbor.

In winter, ice flows freely in the harbor.

A variety of vessels can be found in the slips in the marina.

Wareham

On the north side of the canal, Wareham is contiguous with Bourne and with over 54 miles of coastline has numerous harbors and marinas. At the head of Buzzards Bay, Wareham waters border the channel of the canal. In the 1660s, the local natives sold their lands to the Plymouth Colony to be used for grazing. The abundance of herring and oysters provided sustenance for the early settlers. With the discovery of bog ore, nails, ironware, and farm implements could be manufactured. By the 1820s cut nail factories were constructed to manufacture these products. Only one remains today and has the distinction of being one of the oldest operating industrial buildings in America. Before the building of the canal, areas of Wareham became popular tourist destinations because of the protected harbors and sandy beaches. Gingerbread cottages built in the 1800s were commonplace along the waterfront in Onset.

Now, Wareham attracts numerous visitors with its marinas, protected waterways, and amenities for the beach goers. Access to Buzzards Bay and the Cape Cod Canal make the waters of Wareham attractive to a variety of boaters.

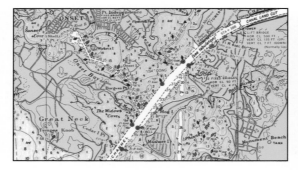

With the white canal channel to the right, the Onset section of Wareham and its connecting waters is to the left. *Courtesy of NOAA.*

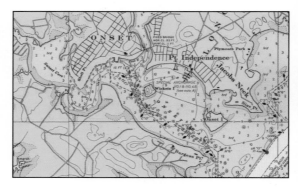

A closer view of Onset with Wicket's Island and the East River leading north and the vistas that can be seen in other images. *Courtesy of NOAA.*

These two towers on Route 28 welcome visitors to Wareham and Cape Cod.

Boats moored in Buttermilk Bay navigate on waters shared by Bourne and Wareham.

The short town pier in Onset.

This Native American statue sits in a park overlooking the town pier and Wicket's Island in the background.

From the same bluff, this old postcard shows Onset Harbor.

A marina along the East River.

A tour boat tied up at the pier offers canal cruises.

Along the East River with a gingerbread designed hotel in the background.

The same river early on a winter morning.

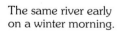

Gingerbread cottages can be found along the Onset shoreline.

These two scenes are of waterways and moorings in Wareham.

Martha's Vineyard

Located seven miles off the south coast of Cape Cod, Martha's Vineyard is almost 90 square miles in size and is comprised of six towns: Chilmark, Edgartown, Aquinnah (Gay Head), Oak Bluffs, Tisbury, and West Tisbury. The island may have been visited as early as 1000 A.D. by the Vikings, but Bartholomew Gosnold, who visited in 1602 and explored other areas of the Cape, is credited with naming it Martha after his daughter. Because of the abundance of grapes, Gosnold called the island Martha's Vineyard. Surrounded by the sea and with two large natural harbors—Vineyard Haven and Edgartown—the island has had a long and storied maritime history. The first English settlers arrived in the mid-1600s to set up a colony in what is now Edgartown. Relations with the Indians were excellent, and many were taught at a school established in 1651. The Indians were the first whalers and claimed any dead whale that washed upon the shore. Many Indians were also crewmembers on the coastal whalers because of their skill in managing the boats. At the height of the whaling industry, one captain was able to kill 7-8 whales per month. As the supply of whales decreased, ships were obliged to travel further out to sea. The first whaler to leave the Vineyard was the schooner *Lydia* in 1765. By the mid-1800s Vineyard ships could be found on all oceans.

In the mid-1830s, the first camp meeting or religious revival was held in what is now Oak Bluffs. As the camp meeting became popular, more people attended, and ships, and later steamers, would bring the visitors. As the other Vineyard harbors developed as a result of fishing and whaling, Oak Bluffs harbor was created to serve maritime activities associated with the town. Of the original piers in

Vineyard Sound, one remains that still docks ferries from the mainland. The inner Oak Bluffs harbor is now primarily used by recreational vessels.

Now, the harbors of the Vineyard that once were lined with whalers and coastal schooners are the ports of mega yachts and hundreds of recreational craft. Oak Bluffs, with its shops, nightlife, and the Campground, attracts boaters who make reservations for slips more than a year in advance. Vineyard Haven is a busy, active harbor with ferries, fishing boats, marinas, and a yacht club. Edgartown attracts touring yacht clubs with its large deep-water facilities. Shoreside, elegant restaurants and galleries await the boaters.

Menemsha, on the southwest side of the island, is probably the smallest of the Vineyard harbors, but provides boaters with all necessary requirements as well as the ambience of an active fishing village. Martha's Vineyard is a boater's paradise, with a harbor that will fit each visitor's needs.

Vineyard Haven

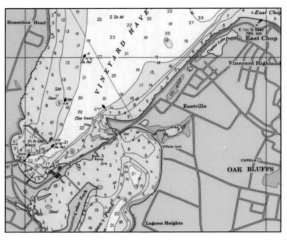

A more recent chart showing the inner harbor and channel. Notice the breakwater that protects moored craft in the harbor. *Courtesy of NOAA.*

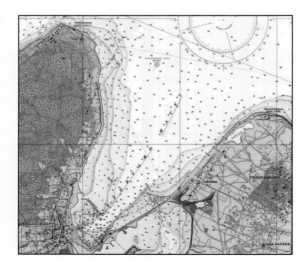

Over 100 years old, this chart shows the Vineyard Haven harbor and the two lighthouses that mark its entrance. At the top left is West Chop, and at the top right is East Chop. Notice that the older charts identified buildings on the land. *Courtesy of NOAA.*

Large sailboats tied up near the ferry dock.

A full moon rises over Vineyard Haven.

The ferry dock with the town's distinctive steeples in the background.

This hundred year old postcard illustrates
the fate of old schooners.

203

Thick fog surrounds boats in the harbor.

Large sailing craft can still be found in the harbor.

West Chop Lighthouse with the waters of Vineyard
Sound in the background.

East Chop Lighthouse is still an active aid to navigation and guides
mariners into both Vineyard Haven and Oak Bluffs.

Lake Tashmoo, found on the northwest coast of the Vineyard, has numerous vessels moored in the waters.

Oak Bluffs

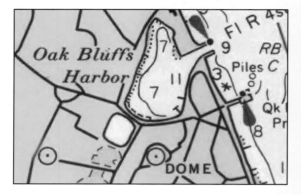

A chart of Oak Bluffs Harbor, which is man-made, and the Camp Meeting attraction. The dome is the Tabernacle found in the Campground. *Courtesy of NOAA.*

From the walkway of East Chop Lighthouse, a ferry can be seen heading into Oak Bluffs.

An old postcard shows the pier that brought steamers loaded with visitors to Oak Bluffs.

A sailboat heads out of Oak Bluffs Harbor.

The Tabernacle with the cross and the Wesley Hotel are distinctive landmarks near the harbor.

Dinghies at the dock in the harbor.

A gingerbread cottage marks this harbor as Oak Bluffs.

207

Early morning, looking west across the harbor.

This view of the harbor includes the harbormaster's office on the left.

The Wesley Hotel is found at the inner edge of the harbor.

208

Menemsha Harbor

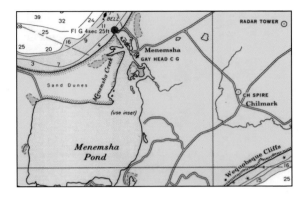

Fishing vessels are tied up at docks with Menemsha Pond in the background.

Located on the southwest coast of Martha's Vineyard and opening on to Vineyard Sound, Menemsha is an active harbor with numerous commercial vessels and a Coast Guard Station. Across the creek where sand dunes are written on the chart is Lobsterville Beach. *Courtesy of NOAA).*

More fishing shacks line Menemsha Creek.

Another view of fishing boats in the harbor. The white building with the red roof is part of the Coast Guard facility.

Near the inlet, the Coast Guard building is prominent. The land in the distance becomes Gay Head with its cliffs and lighthouse.

Beach roses bloom in the spring with Menemsha Creek and the Coast Guard facility in the background.

Traps line the dock waiting to be put in the water.

Town landing on Menemsha Pond.

Ruddy turnstones, in their winter plumage, searching for food.

Inside Gay Head Lighthouse looking west.

Gay Head Lighthouse stands on the cliffs overlooking Vineyard Sound. In the background, the land is part of the Elizabeth Islands.

211

Menemsha beach is a quiet peaceful place to enjoy the water.

This statue of a fisherman harpooning a swordfish stands just behind the beach. Notice the Coast Guard building in the background.

Fishing lures hang in this shack window.

Edgartown Harbor

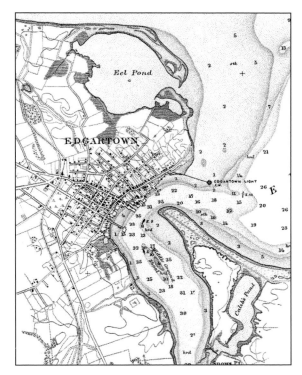

A pre-1900 chart of Edgartown Harbor. Compare the changes that have occurred with the modern chart. Notice the difference with Eel Pond and the location of Edgartown Light. *Courtesy of NOAA.*

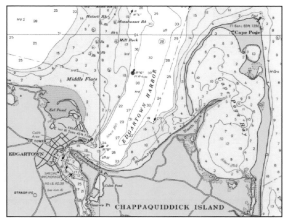

This modern chart shows not only Edgartown Harbor but also Chappaquiddick Island, which is accessed by the "on time" ferry. Cape Poque, only accessible by four-wheel drive vehicles, has a lighthouse at the northern tip of the island.
Courtesy of NOAA.

From the lower level of the town pier, looking South.

A view of the harbor from the town pier.

213

Edgartown Harbor, looking south towards Katama Bay.

The "on time" ferry provides access to Chappaquiddick Island. Edgartown Lighthouse is in the background.

Commercial boats in Edgartown Harbor.

Two views of inner Edgartown Harbor with its boats and buildings.

Two lighthouses assist mariners in navigating Edgartown Harbor. At sunset, Edgartown Light marks the inner harbor.

At the tip of Chappaquiddick Island, Cape Poque Light aids navigators.

215

Nantucket

Thirty miles south of Cape Cod lies Nantucket, also known as the "The Grey Lady," the southern-most community in Massachusetts. It is unique in that the town, the island, and the county are all called Nantucket. Gosnold, whose travels around the Cape in 1602 have been mentioned earlier, described the cliffs of Siasconset as he sailed past. The island was occupied by about 1500 Native Americans when the first English settlers arrived in the late 1650s. Native Americans from other locales would travel to the island on a seasonal basis to fish and search for dead whales that came ashore. Whaling became a major maritime industry, with ships hailing from Nantucket found on oceans around the world. In 1760, Nantucket produced more whale oil than all other ports combined. Readers of *Moby Dick* may remember the "Nantucket sleigh ride," when the line went taut on a harpooned whale and the boat was dragged along the water. Whaleboats could be easily smashed by the leviathans and many men lost their lives in their pursuit. With the whaling success came the mansions built as the Federal, Georgian, and Greek Revival architecture that can still be found on the main streets of the town.

What was for years a quiet peaceful island, Nantucket has become a playground for the rich and famous. With a year-round population of about 10,000, the island swells to over 50,000 during the busy summer season. Where once whalers docked, magnificent large yachts can be found in the harbor. Yacht clubs make Nantucket a must stop on their coastal cruises. Other smaller vessels can be found in slips and moored in a variety of anchorages. Commercial fishing boats are also present. Whether you arrive in your boat or by ferry, Nantucket has something for everyone with restaurants, galleries, museums and shops that are first class.

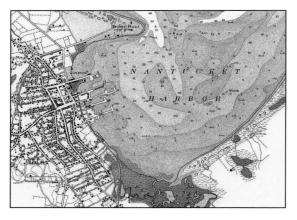

This 1884 chart shows the harbor with the four piers that were once busy with the whaling ships. Brant Point Lighthouse at the top marks the entrance to the harbor and still guides navigators. *Courtesy of NOAA.*

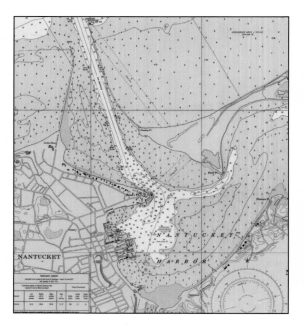

A modern chart of Nantucket Harbor. *Courtesy of NOAA.*

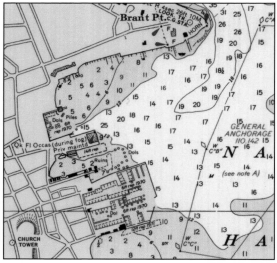

A close up of the piers showing the slips on the lower docks; the upper docks are used by the ferry boats.

Brant Point Lighthouse, on a spit of land on the north side of the harbor, is still an active aid to navigation.

The Coast Guard Station is located behind the lighthouse.

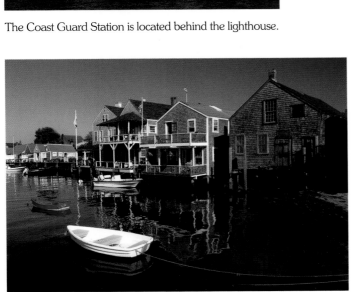

The church is a distinctive landmark for those entering Nantucket Harbor.

A scene along the harbor's edge.

This postcard, over 100 years old, shows a fleet of typical sailboats.

Houses line one of the piers in the harbor.

Nearby Straight Wharf was built in 1723.

This postcard shows a sailing vessel that was commonly found in the harbor over one hundred years ago.

Old South Wharf, built in 1770, now caters to shoppers.

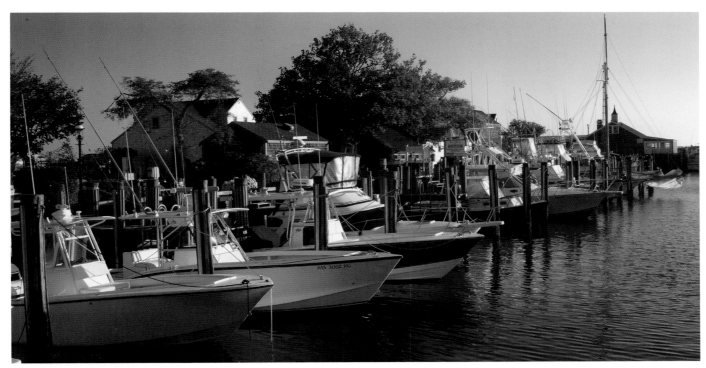

Along the wharf, boats can be found in slips.

Brant Point Light used to be surrounded by water, so the walkway would provide access.

Found along the eastern shore of Nantucket, Sankaty Head Lighthouse provides mariners an active aid to navigation.

North of Sankaty Light, Great Point Lighthouse marks the northeast tip of Nantucket.

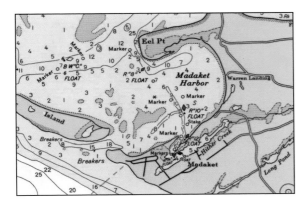

At the far western end of Nantucket, Madaket Harbor provides moorings for smaller recreational craft. *Courtesy of NOAA.*

HITHER CREEK IS A NO WAKE ZONE STRICKLY ENFORCED

Decorated for the holidays, Brant Point has a distinctive red light.

Two views of the boat slips in Madaket Harbor.

A view of the waters of Madaket Harbor.

Conclusion

Four hundred years ago, the harbors of Cape Cod were used by explorers for safety. With the abundance of finfish and shellfish in the nearby waters, there was also an ample supply of food. As more voyagers visited, additional harbors were explored, charted, and mapped. With the Pilgrims and more Europeans settling in the New World, travel across the water was frequently the preferred method to trade goods and visit other colonies. Shipbuilding and other maritime endeavors involved nearly every town on the Cape. Harbors were the center of town activity, with products from the sea being processed and sent to their final destination. Trade between towns with coastal schooners occurred all along the coast. With the building of more roads and the coming of the railroad, trade over the water diminished. With fluctuations and a decline in fishing stocks, harbors no longer had as many ships. With the collapse of the whaling industry, shipbuilding and other activities were no longer required; harbors were no longer bustling and many fell into decline.

Today, the waters and harbors of Cape Cod are bustling with activity again and the variety of vessels is extensive. Many of the larger ports have a significant number of commercial boats involved in fishing and clamming. But now, more than ever before, recreational powerboats and sailboats are the most common vessels in a harbor. Some harbors have so many boats, that craft not being used are stored in racks. The demands for space within several harbors are at all time highs and waiting lists are for double-digit years. The waters of Cape Cod, Martha's Vineyard, and Nantucket are pristine with recreational boaters cruising, sailing, and enjoying this region.

Bibliography

Farson, Robert H. *The Cape Cod Canal.* Cape Cod Historical Publications, Yarmouthport, Massachusetts. 1987

Powell, Lyman P. *Historic Towns of New England.* G.P. Putnam's New York, The Knickerbocker Press, 1899.

Robinson, William F. *Coastal New England, Its Life and Past.* New York Graphic Society, Boston. 1983.

Strahler, Arthur N. *A Geologist's View of Cape Cod.* Parnassus Imprints, 1988.

Weeden, William B. *Economic and Social History of New England Vol II.* Houghton, Mifflin and Company, The University Press, 1890.

Wilensky, Julius M. *CAPE COD, Where to go, What to do, How to do it.* Wescott Cove Publishing Company, Stamford Connecticut. 1969.

www.wikipedia.com and the numerous links found on the communities.

Index

ANSWERS

1. Provincetown Harbor; 2. Woods Hole Harbor; 3. Hyannis Harbor; 4. Bass River, Dennis/Yarmouth; 5. Arey's Pond, Orleans; 6. Chase Garden Creek, Dennis/Yarmouth; 7. Mill Pond, Chatham; 8. Mill Pond, Orleans; 9. Herring River, Harwich; 10. The Knob, Quisset Harbor, Falmouth; 11. Ockway Bay, Mashpee; 12. Pamet River and Harbor, Truro; 13. Wychmere Harbor, Harwichport; 14. Prince Cove, Marstons Mills; 15. Wellfleet Harbor; 16. Pleasant Bay, Chatham; 17. Onset; 18. Snug Harbor, West Falmouth; 19. Stage harbor, Chatham; 20. Paw Wah Pond, South Orleans